The Influencer Secrets to Success and Happiness

BRIAN AHEARN

CPCU, CTM, CPT, CMCT

Printed in the United States of America
Interior Layout Design by Standout Books

ISBN (paperback): 978-1-7331785-4-9
ISBN (ebook): 978-1-7331785-5-6

Contents

Praise for *The Influencer*

"With The Influencer, Brian Ahearn provides an especially resonant narrative of its major character's growing mastery of the influence process, which offers readers fresh and accumulating evidence of how social influence works. All the while, he details ways to profitably implement these new understandings to become more influential. It's a tour de force."

– Robert B. Cialdini, Ph.D., President of INFLUENCE AT WORK, author of *Influence* and *Pre-Suasion*

"Brian Ahearn has crafted a story about John Andrews, a perceptive, middle-class young man who goes off to college and takes a psychology class that lights a fire, kindling his mind throughout his life and career. This is a book for anyone in a position of influence! You will be a better teacher, coach, manager, leader, salesperson, or elected official, when you learn how to use the scientifically proven methods of persuasion Brian shares throughout the book."

– Todd Alles, former Director of Football Operations at the University of Alabama and The Ohio State University

"The Influencer: Secrets to Success and Happiness allows the reader to join the main character in a heartfelt journey of understanding his own influence. The Influencer outlines the subtle-but-profound gems of wisdom that are available to all of us over the arc of our lives, if we are *paying attention to our experiences. The relationships, circumstances, and life events the main character lives through encourage all of us to take note of how much we are learning about ourselves, and each other, along the way. The Influencer reflects on a life well-lived, and offers clear, useful lessons on the psychology of influence."*

– Daniel Stover, M.A., Founder & CEO, Ensight Partners

"The science of persuasion is academic and clear. The art of persuasion is nuanced. If you follow the science in an artful way, you WILL become more persuasive and influential. How do you do this? Follow the story of John Andrews. If your job involves any persuasion and influence (hint: all jobs do) the story of John Andrews, an ordinary person who becomes an extraordinary influencer, will give you a new roadmap for professional and personal success. If you're someone who actually sells (in the elegant and beneficial way we talk about sales), go immediately to your favorite book vendor and add The Influencer: Secrets to Success and Happiness to your must-read list."

– Becki Saltzman, Founder & Chief Curiosity
Seeker, Applied Curiosity Lab

"I love what Brian did using the storytelling format to teach readers about influence. He takes you through so many different situations you're likely to encounter during your personal life and career. The book is a fun, easy read that will help anyone who wants to be more influential!"

– Bas Wouters, CMCT, CEO, Online Influence
Institute, and co-author of *Online Influence*

"Brian Ahearn has distilled his vast knowledge about persuasion, and ways to use this knowledge for good, in an easy to read and understandable story. No matter the sector, the principles of persuasion are well-researched, proven, and effective. Brian shares a

narrative that makes the principles of persuasion relevant to everyday life and demonstrates the multitude of ways they can be applied in professional and personal situations."

– Christy Farnbauch, Executive Director, Contemporary
American Theatre Company, Columbus, Ohio

"Brian Ahearn is a Social Scientist. He is Social because enjoys, understands, and deeply appreciates relationships. He is a Scientist in that Brian happens to be in a small minority of individuals certified to unpack the science of Robert Cialdini's Principles of Ethical Influence. The Influencer beautifully displays the insights of Relational Brian Ahearn, while unfolding the Scientist Brian Ahearn ~ I guarantee you will, as I have, benefit from this read and this man."

– Dennis Stranges, Ph.D., Executive Coach and
Founder of Insight Coaching & Consulting

"Written in a format that is both approachable and memorable, Brian Ahearn tackles a topic critical to leaders at every level. Not only does influence matter, but doing it in the right way for the right reasons matters even more. Ahearn gets this and delivers a message that hits the mark."

– Jamie Leddin, Director of The Leddin Group,
Lecturer at Vanderbilt University

"Brian Ahearn has written a wonderful book that is sure to help anyone who is interested in leadership or sales. In order to become successful in either of these fields, the ability to influence others is vital to your success. This book, written in an entertaining and well-organized style, provides a roadmap for doing just that. I highly recommend this book!"

– Steven L. Anderson, Ph.D., MBA, President
of Integrated Leadership Systems

"*This book is a must-read for anyone who wishes to reach higher levels of success. In today's world, the ability to understand and effectively influence is a vital skill. Brian has outdone himself in The Influencer by teaching us how to learn and utilize the skills of influence. He presents these valuable life lessons in a manner that aids in remembering and implementing the tools he gives us.*"

– Gail Rudolph, CMCT, CFRE, Founder and CEO, Gail Rudolph Collaborative, Author of *Power Up Power Down*

Foreword

Thirteen pages, size twelve font, single-spaced. Thirteen pages!

That describes the vast amount of notes I had after reading Brian Ahearn's first book, *Influence PEOPLE: Powerful Everyday Opportunities to Persuade that are Lasting and Ethical.* Over the last decade I've had the honor of facilitating thousands of negotiation and conflict resolution training sessions. I've taught at the MBA level at Otterbein University in Columbus, Ohio, and at the law-school level for The Ohio State University Moritz College of Law. Even with all my years of teaching AND learning, there is something truly special that happens *every time* I read one of Brian's books. Turning that last page, I am full of fresh ideas that are both new and exciting. I emerge re-energized and eager to apply my newfound knowledge to my personal quest to change the world with the tools of negotiation.

Brian has been a mentor, colleague, and close friend for years. We've had several amazing conversations about life, love, and the pursuit of happiness. It's been my pleasure to have him on my podcast, *Negotiate Anything*, four times; the only guest speaker to be invited back so frequently. Now we've been fortunate to have some truly incredible thought leaders on the program, including Chris Voss and Alexandra Carter, but Brian is always a standout. I continue to invite him back because I know my audience can glean an invaluable amount of wisdom from his engagement.

I've read a lot of books, and I've even been fortunate enough to write one myself. In all my time I haven't seen anybody approach the skills of negotiation, persuasion, and success quite like Brian does, and certainly not in the narrative format. Upon hearing of his idea for *The Influencer: Secrets to Success and Happiness*, I immediately knew it was brilliant and having had the opportunity to preview the book (thanks for the special sneak peek friend) I can honestly say it exceeded my expectations, a feat I didn't believe was possible. Brian has found a way to bring his teachings to life, expanding beyond the traditionally featured case study often included in the majority of the books in the market. He's managed to condense a lifetime of potential and opportunity into one book, allowing the reader to study the entirety of one's life, rather than a snapshot of one moment in time.

It's important to remember that the skills Brian highlights aren't just for business, they are life skills that can truly elevate all aspects of your current reality. Our market has been long overdue for a book like this; one that really exemplifies how you can apply the skills of negotiation, persuasion, and influence in practical ways that will not only enhance your life, but the lives of those around you.

If it hasn't been said already, this book is absolutely 100% life-changing! Coaches, trainers, and authors often use the word "life-changing" to describe the wisdom they seek to impart to their audience, so why should you believe me? Because while I think everybody who reads books on negotiation, communication, and persuasion can conceptualize just how the teachings will positively influence their life or career, using the full life of John (the protagonist) really breaks down how these specific skills can be applied to any and ALL seasons of our journey.

At the American Negotiation Institute, we believe that the best things in life are on the other side of difficult conversations. In all my years of learning and teaching in this industry, I've yet to come across a piece of literature that exemplifies that belief more than this book.

Knowing what lies ahead for you as the reader, I can't overstate how excited I am to see how this book impacts your life. If your experience is anything like mine, you are truly about to embark on an incredible journey so keep a thick notebook handy.

  – Kwame Christian, Esq., M.A., is the author of *Finding Confidence in Conflict*, the host of Negotiate Anything (the #1 negotiation podcast in the world!), and Director of the American Negotiation Institute.

Brian Ahearn

Brian Ahearn is the founder of Influence PEOPLE, LLC. An international speaker, trainer, coach, and consultant, he helps clients apply the science of influence to ensure more professional success at the office and personal happiness at home.

Brian was personally trained by Robert B. Cialdini, Ph.D., the most cited living social psychologist on the planet when it comes to the science of ethical influence and persuasion. Brian is one of only a dozen individuals in the world who currently holds the coveted Cialdini Method Certified Trainer (CMCT) designation, and he is one of just a handful who've earned the Cialdini Pre-suasion Trainer (CPT) designation.

Influence PEOPLE: Powerful Everyday Opportunities to Persuade that are Lasting and Ethical was Brian's first book. Not only was it an Amazon bestseller, it was also named one of the Top 100 Influence Books of All Time by BookAuthority.

Brian's second book, *Persuasive Selling for Relationship Driven Insurance Agents*, was an Amazon new release bestseller.

A LinkedIn Learning author, Brian's courses on applying influence in sales and coaching have been viewed by more than 400,000 people across the globe.

When Brian isn't influencing people he enjoys reading, traveling, working out, good Scotch, and spending time with his wife Jane. Together Brian and Jane have one daughter, Abigail, who is an American Sign Language (ASL) interpreter.

Looking for a speaker for your next event?

Connect with Brian on LinkedIn: https://www.linkedin.com/in/brianfahearn/

Visit Brian's website: https://www.influencepeople.biz

Email Brian at Brian.Ahearn@influencepeople.biz

Preface

I've been blogging weekly for more than a dozen years and have written nearly 700 blog posts. I've written countless articles over my career and have authored two books on influence. That's a lot of writing which makes my next statement even more significant; I've never had as much fun writing as I did with this book!

My first book, *Influence PEOPLE: Powerful Everyday Opportunities to Persuade that are Lasting and Ethical*, is a business/psychology book written for people who don't want to get mired down in detailed psychological studies. The book hits the high points of the psychology of persuasion with a focus on application. In it I share easy to implement ideas anyone can use immediately. I was thrilled when it became an Amazon bestseller. I was blown away when it was named one of the *Top 100 Influence Books of All Time* by BookAuthority.

My second book was *Persuasive Selling for Relationship Driven Insurance Agents*. As the title conveys, it's a sales book that's geared towards a particular market. I decided to focus on what I knew best – insurance and sales – because I'd spent more than 30 years working for insurance companies and with independent insurance agents. The book looks at the sales process and helps insurance agents understand which psychology is best at different points along the sales cycle. It also teaches readers influence approaches for dealing with different personality styles.

Knowing many people will never pick up a psychology or a sales book, I decided to write *The Influencer* as a business parable to help a new set of readers understand how to ethically influence people. As youngsters, we loved stories. Stories as a way of learning go all the way back to the beginning of human history. Knowing this, I thought, "Why not write a story almost anyone can relate to that shows how influence can be used at work and home to enjoy more success and happiness?"

As I wrote *The Influencer: Secrets to Success and Happiness* I thought of stories I've enjoyed that taught me profound lessons. *The Richest Man in Babylon*, *The Alchemist*, *Joshua: A Parable for Today*, and *The Go-Giver*, are a few favorites that come to mind. If my book is remotely considered along with those classics I'll be thrilled.

The Influencer follows the life and career of John Andrews. During his freshman year of college he takes a psychology course that ultimately impacts the rest of his life. As he moves into his career and goes through training, interacts with clients, works with coaches and mentors, and forms personal relationships, the people he meets along the way teach him valuable lessons about business and life. He starts putting together everything he's learning and sees it as a puzzle to be solved. The lessons form a picture which becomes his approach to life, dealing with people, and ultimately success and happiness.

As I wrote the book some people asked if it's my story I'm telling. Bits and pieces are based on my personal experiences. For example, I did take a psychology class as a freshman at Miami University and among all my college courses, it was my most memorable. However, John Andrews' life is more charmed than mine because he learns important truths much sooner than I did and he is more proactive about implementing what he learns.

Having shared that bits and pieces are based on some of my personal experiences, I have to say that one of the most enjoyable aspects about writing this book was an opportunity to think back on people who've impacted my career and life; family, bosses, coaches, role models, friends, and countless others. I was able to incorporate many of them into the book as my way of thanking them for the impact they had on me. Whether or not they realized it at the time, they taught me valuable lessons which I can now share with others. To see who those people are and the characters I modeled after them, go to the Acknowledgements section at the end of the book.

Since this book is about influence, happiness, and success, I want to quickly share my views on each.

When it comes to influence, I see it as the ability to impact another person's heart, mind, and behavior. Influence encompasses how we communicate, carry ourselves, and who we are. Aristotle put it well when he said, "Character may almost be called the most effective means of persuasion." Influence entails what we do before, during, and after we attempt to persuade others.

Success is something each of us gets to define ourselves. For some, success is climbing the corporate ladder. Others believe it's the sense of accomplishment knowing you've done your best. Hearing yes to our ideas and proposals is a large part of achieving professional success.

Like success, happiness is a concept each of us also defines. What makes me happy may not make you happy and vice versa. There's no universal set point for happiness but you know it when you experience it. In my first book, *Influence PEOPLE*, the final chapter was The Key to Happiness. The secret I shared was simple – ***Happy is the person who wants what they have***. I encourage you to ponder that. It's key because when you focus on what you have with gratitude, you will be happier.

With that, I hope you enjoy *The Influencer*, learn new influence approaches as you read, and that ultimately you'll reap the rewards of success and happiness as a result.

In the Beginning...

The Andrews Home

All good stories start with "In the beginning," and this one is no exception. You cannot fully appreciate what's happening in the moment if you don't understand how you got to where you are. Knowing that, it's necessary to go back to the beginning to understand John Andrews.

John, or "Johnny" as he was affectionately called by his mother and father, was born into a typical middle class American family. Aside from that bit of good fortune, there were no special circumstances surrounding his birth, much like the vast majority of humans. His arrival brought joy to his family but beyond that, his entrance into the world was pretty much like the billions of people who came before him. That's to say, he wasn't born under a favorable star, angels didn't announce his arrival, nor did wisemen or dignitaries visit his family soon after his birth. Perhaps the most notable fact about John's coming forth party was that it took place on St. Patrick's Day.

In addition to John, the Andrews children consisted of an older brother and sister. Billy was five years old and Carey was two when John came home from the hospital. They were both excited to meet their baby brother. Billy wanted a boy to play ball with and Carey wanted a baby to hold, dress up, and play with.

John's parents, Todd and Jane, made up the rest of the relatively normal middle class American family. Todd was an accountant for a large firm where he regularly worked 50-hour weeks and considerably more during tax season. Throughout college Todd had dreams of becoming a corporate executive. He met Jane just as both were about to graduate. Landing jobs in the same city allowed them to explore their relationship more than would have been possible had they ended up in different parts of the country.

Todd was a serious minded individual and quickly decided office politics were not for him. Just like numbers either added up or they didn't, most things were black and white, right or wrong for Todd. Office politics fell into the wrong category because he felt advancement, raises, and bonuses were not always based on merit. This offended his sense of fairness and that's when he let go of the dream of becoming a high-level executive. He felt it was unattainable unless he went against his conscience. While that's certainly not the case with every organization, it happened to be the situation where Todd worked.

Despite the office politics, Todd genuinely liked his job and enjoyed most of his coworkers. By the time John arrived Todd had been with the company for nearly a decade. He was well paid and had good benefits. With three children under the age of five, and college to save for, Todd wasn't looking to make a career change. If change was to happen, it would have to come looking for him and whatever was offered would have to come with guarantees because the older Todd got the more risk averse he became. There was simply too much on the line for his family.

Jane had studied marketing during college and took a job with a small advertising agency shortly after graduating. The pay wasn't great, but she enjoyed everything about the job, and it allowed her to stay close to Todd. They married a few years after graduation and she continued to work full time, even after the birth of Billy. It wasn't until Carey came along that she began to rethink her career. Todd was doing well and was thrifty with their money so they knew they could afford to have her work part time which would allow her to devote more time and energy to the kids. When she became pregnant with John they started talking about having her stay home full time because, as Todd aptly pointed out, anything she made working part time would be chewed up by childcare costs after taxes. They both thought, why work just to pay someone else to raise our kids?

So, they tightened their budget, watched their pennies closely and began a new family phase as Jane transitioned to a full-time mom when she came home from the hospital with John. Of course, Billy and Carey loved having mom around all the time and seeing her at school functions made them feel special.

School Years

Grade school, middle school, and high school were somewhat uneventful for John. Although well-liked by his classmates, he didn't stand out in any significant way. He wasn't at the top of his class when it came to grades, but he was a solid B student.

He played several sports growing up and, while he was athletic, he was by no means a superstar. In high school he started to take golf more seriously and made the golf team as a junior and senior. Golf became somewhat of a passion for John and he liked that it was something he could do apart from organized sports.

John dated a little during his junior and senior years but there were no serious relationships. He would have pursued dating a little more if he'd been more self-assured. Like many teenagers, he felt awkward when it came to asking someone out and the fear of rejection loomed large. Consequently, he remained content hanging out with his buddies most weekends.

He participated in a few clubs but was never one to volunteer for leadership roles. There were no sports or academic scholarships to be had so it was good that his dad was a planner. Todd had started saving for each child's college education as soon as they were born.

By the time John was ready for college Billy had already finished school. He moved out of state to take a job as a financial planner within weeks of graduation. Carey, although only two years older than John, would finish college sooner than expected because of accelerated high school classes that earned her college credits and an aggressive class schedule in her first few years of college. This was good news for the family because paying for college tuition for three kids at the same time would have been a huge strain on their finances, even with Todd's planning.

Off to College

John went to an in-state university a few hours from his hometown. It was far enough to be away but close enough to get home whenever he needed to. He loved the feel of college; the large stone and brick buildings, the ivy that crept up the old walls, and the informal walkways students wore into the grass as they took the shortest paths possible from one building to another.

Whenever there was a home football or basketball game the campus came alive with parties. You could hardly go anywhere without hearing screams and laughter. Even when neither team was having a good season it didn't matter because games were an excuse to gather and have more fun than usual.

As John started his college experience he began to take more notice of the people around him. He recognized this was a brand-new start with people he'd never met before. He could be whomever he wanted to be and become whatever he wanted to become. The problem was, he didn't have a clue as to what he wanted to do, let alone who he wanted to be. Nonetheless, his newfound awareness was good and it prompted him to start thinking differently about the future.

Like so many freshmen trying to figure out what they wanted to do, John enrolled in some basic classes to fulfill general requirements and started his academic journey. One class he particularly enjoyed was Psych 101. This course was a staple for incoming students who didn't know what their major was going to be. It was so popular that 200+ students regularly filled the huge stadium seated auditorium every Monday, Wednesday, and Friday mornings at 9:00 a.m. and 11:00 a.m. Unfortunately, too many looked at it as a throw away class, something to take simply to get four hours of college credit. However, a few students like John realized when you're dealing with people, it all comes down to psychology. John figured the more he understood how people thought and behaved, the easier it would be for him to communicate with people, no matter how much they differed from him.

Truthfully, his first thoughts about applying whatever he learned in the psych class revolved around dating. His lack of dating during high school was partly due to his introverted nature coupled with an ever-present nervousness around girls. Quite often that combination left him fumbling for words. He felt understanding the human mind might help him overcome his shy side and land him a few more dates without all the anxiety that comes with the territory. As the psych course progressed he started to realize what he was learning might also help him get along better with friends and family; perhaps negotiate a better grade with teachers; and might come in handy when he reached the end of college and started interviewing for jobs. That final thought didn't loom too large because the four years till graduation seemed like an eternity.

What fascinated him most about Psych 101 was the time spent on something called "the science of influence." He'd heard his dad use that word – influence – on occasion but it was usually in a negative way. He recalled hearing him say over dinner one evening, "Joe tried to influence me to go along with his lame idea to restructure the department." He also overheard him tell his mom about other changes taking place at work, "I'm not going to be influenced by some talking head who has no idea what we do in our department." John's first impressions of influence were tied to manipulation. Did influence mean talking someone into something they didn't want to do?

However, this negative impression was countered by John's classroom and other exposures to the word. There was a book he'd heard mentioned a few times on television and radio interviews: Dale Carnegie's *How to Win Friends and Influence People*. When it came to those references the word influence was positive because he remembered people saying the book changed their lives for the better.

During the psych course one of the required readings was *Influence: The Psychology of Persuasion* by Robert Cialdini, Ph.D. What fascinated John was the research cited in the book to back up the claims of effectiveness. He'd seen late night infomercials for motivational speakers, men and women who would pump up audiences and make big claims about success, but John always wondered how effective their methods were, especially for those who bought their courses or attended their conferences. When reading *Influence* there was no doubt about the effectiveness because every claim in the book was backed up by decades of research from social psychology. What stood out to John was how seemingly small changes – simply adding a word like "because" when giving a reason, paying attention to what comes after "but" in a sentence, and asking instead of telling – could make such a huge difference in people's willingness to say yes.

John made sure to note the most important concepts. He even wrote them down and posted them on the wall next to his dorm room desk to serve as a reminder. Here's what he wrote:

- Liking – If people like you they'll say yes to you.
- Unity – People you share a deep connection with are more likely to say yes to you.
- Reciprocity – Be a giver if you ever hope to get.
- Social Proof – Talk about what other people are doing.
- Authority – If an expert says it, people are more likely to believe it.
- Consistency – People feel good about themselves when they keep their word.
- Scarcity – People respond to the fear of missing out.
- Contrast – Make good comparisons so people notice differences.

- Because – Give reasons using "because" and people will be more likely to do what you want.

John's attempts at using the psychology he was learning were hit or miss. He didn't realize it at first but trying to influence people's thinking and behavior was a skill and, as is the case with most skills, there's a learning curve. Then he began to tie everything back to something familiar: golf. He still played and would take lessons whenever his game started to slip. He remembered whatever the golf pro had him do – adjust his grip, change his stance, work on keeping his elbow in – felt awkward at first. In fact, he usually hit the ball worse as he attempted to put into practice the tips the pro taught. It was frustrating but eventually he would start to hit the ball better if he kept at it. As he thought about his golf lessons he noticed the parallel when attempting to use the influence concepts he was learning.

As he put his learning into practice he found dating was less anxiety producing than it had been in high school. That was primarily because he made sure to talk about what he had in common with whomever he was dating. In the past he would have focused on himself without concern for his date. It wasn't that he was self-absorbed, he just felt comfortable talking about his interests and hobbies.

He also went out of his way to pay genuine compliments. His dates could sense his sincerity and their subsequent smiles and laughter put John at ease. While his new approach opened more dating opportunities, he never had a serious relationship during college. He was content just meeting new people.

It wasn't all sunshine and roses when it came to applying what he learned in the psych class. One blunder included asking for a big favor right on the heels of having helped a friend. He overheard Tom mentioning in class that he needed information to finish a term paper so John volunteered to help Tom. As soon as he gave Tom what he needed he immediately asked to borrow his car. That request seemed to make Tom feel like John's help wasn't authentic, only a way to get him to do John a favor. He noticed Tom and a few others started avoiding him.

He was getting better at asking instead of telling but this led to a new problem. What if someone said no? Not knowing how to handle rejection put him in the same awkward state he'd experienced when dating in high school. He usually answered somewhat awkwardly, "Okay, thanks," then left the situation feeling a little deflated.

One other mistake he made was coming across as a negative person occasionally, almost a fear monger, when attempting to employ scarcity. People might respond to loss but they don't want to feel threatened or scared into taking some action. He also focused too much on what was at stake for him, rather than the other person. Truth be told, when it comes to what might be lost, most people care more about their own interests than those of the other person.

This learning was par for the course, but it did give John pause to wonder if the psychology stuff was as effective as the research seemed to indicate.

When his freshman year ended he packed up his belongings and headed home. His thoughts revolved around just a few activities: relaxing, working a part time summer job, and hanging out with friends. Like so many students on summer break, he put that first year of college in the rearview mirror and didn't think about school until about a week before it was time to return in the fall.

John's next three years were typical of the college experience: making new friends, going to parties, learning more than he realized, and growing in independence. "Out of sight, out of mind" would be the best way to describe his Psych 101 experience because there was so much demanding his immediate attention from his course load. When he unpacked his belongings each of the next three years, he never put up his psych notes as he had his freshman year. As a result, the concepts were mostly relegated to the back of his mind along with so much else he learned.

During his senior year he really buckled down on his studies because he wanted to achieve a grade point above 3.5 so he could graduate cum laude. During the final month of his last semester he started getting ready for job interviews. Although he was a business major with a minor in marketing, he didn't really know what he wanted to do. Like so many young people he dreamed of making it big quickly. His dreams included traveling the country and maybe the world someday. Those aspirations would take money so he paid close attention to salaries when checking out interview opportunities. He decided the best route to his goals would be getting some type of sales job. He reasoned that his success would rest primarily with himself. If he worked for a good company with solid products or services he thought he would do well. Truthfully, he knew nothing about what it would take to succeed in sales but his intuition about self-reliance was spot on. Success would depend more on him – his desire to grow professionally and personally, a drive to succeed at whatever he did, a willingness to learn, and the courage to try new approaches – than anything else.

As his final semester was winding down John started getting rid of items he wouldn't need after school, like old textbooks and notebooks. While going through his belongings he came across the Psych 101 notes he'd hung on the wall during his freshman year. He looked at what he'd written:

- Liking – If people like you they'll say yes to you.
- Unity – People you share a deep connection with are more likely to say yes to you.
- Reciprocity – Be a giver if you ever hope to get.
- Social Proof – Talk about what other people are doing.
- Authority – If an expert says it, people are more likely to believe it.
- Consistency – People feel good about themselves when they keep their word.
- Scarcity – People respond to the fear of missing out.
- Contrast – Make good comparisons so people notice differences.
- Because – Give reasons using "because" and people will be more likely to do what you want.

As he prepared for his upcoming interviews he saw an opportunity to try the psychology again. He reasoned he had nothing to lose and perhaps a lot to gain. Knowing a job was on the line he asked one of his roommates to do a few mock interviews with him. The "interviews" usually degenerated into laughter before too long, but they did help John focus on what he might say to obvious questions.

During the interviews he was less nervous than he thought he would be. The nerves seemed to melt away once the conversations started and John found them enjoyable. In addition to focusing on what he had in common with the people who interviewed him, he made sure to offer compliments when warranted, just as he'd done with dates. He let each interviewer know that he believed psychology was critical for understanding people and how it was the foundation of sales.

He participated in a half dozen interviews and to his surprise was offered three positions. In each case the interviewers said they were impressed with his likable personality. *His attempts to engage liking by finding common ground and giving sincere compliments paid off.* Each person told him he wouldn't get anywhere in sales if current and prospective customers didn't like him. Since he was so likable, they figured they could teach him everything else he needed to learn.

The choice was difficult because each company and what they offered seemed so good. To help with the decision he turned to his dad. He knew his dad's logical approach to life and business would help him think through all that needed to be weighed in his first big decision as an adult.

He settled on a medical supply company, MediTech Supplies, located in Charlotte, North Carolina. The company wasn't huge but had big plans for the future. Since its inception fifteen years ago the company had grown from 10 employees to more than 100. Given the growing older population and focus on health care in the country the company expected to double in size every five years. Most of the executives had decades of experience in the industry and had come over from much larger competitors because of the growth opportunity they saw at MediTech.

John liked the executives he met during his interviews at the Med-iTech headquarters. He felt like they were regular people who really wanted each employee to succeed. Considering the company was still small he saw this as an opportunity to get to know the decision makers in ways he couldn't at a bigger company. He was determined to take them up on their offers to help him however they could. John also liked the company's focus on employee growth. In addition to in-house training they budgeted for salespeople to attend a couple of conferences each year and to take some outside training.

The Trainee

Although John enjoyed the two months off between graduation and starting his first job, he was chomping at the bit to begin this new phase of life. College had been fun but by the time he was a senior he'd had his fill of campus life and everything that goes with it. Seeing friends who'd started their careers made him a bit envious. They had new cars, nice apartments, and some were traveling.

It was mid-July when John walked into MediTech headquarters as a trainee. The front of the three-story building was mostly glass and the morning sun lit up the entire lobby, giving a pleasant feel to start the day. The workday started at 8:00 a.m. but the trainees were told to arrive at 8:30 a.m. so everything would be ready for their first day. The atmosphere of the corporate headquarters was exciting and a little overwhelming initially. There was a buzz about the place as people hurried to and from meetings. Despite the hectic pace it was a friendly atmosphere as people walked by and said hello to one another.

The company put him and five other sales trainees up in apartments for three months. They would all go through an eight-week training program then spend a month shadowing various salespeople before getting their territory assignments. John's assignment could land him anywhere in the country and he was excited about the

possibilities. He'd spent his entire life in the Midwest and wanted to
see more of the country.

The training would focus on teaching him and the others about
the industry, the company, their products and services, their ideal
customers, and basic selling skills.

While three months of training seemed like it would be a long time,
especially from the perspective of a 22-year-old, it flew by. Everything
was new – the city, the company, the people he met, the places he
went, what he was learning – and that seemed to speed up everything. John and the other trainees felt like they were drinking from
a firehose. At least in college there were breaks between classes, but
this learning was 8:00 a.m. to 5:00 p.m. followed by at least an hour
of study every night. He felt like a whole year of college was crammed
into those few months of training.

Fortunately, John loved everything about the experience. Unlike
many college courses, he knew what he was learning at MediTech
would be directly applicable to his role as a sales rep. Just as he'd done
with his Psych 101 course, John wrote down the highlights of what he
was learning. This time he used yellow sticky notes that he strategi-
cally placed around his apartment and office. They served as visual
reminders of what he needed to keep front and center. Below is what
stood out to John. What he wrote on his sticky notes are in italicized
font followed by his interpretation of the message.

- *Is this a career or just a job?* He needed to decide because there
  was a big difference. Approaching his new role at MediTech
  as a career, not just a job, was as different as approaching
  something as a passion instead of a hobby. He knew he would
  pour more time, energy, and effort into a passion over a hobby.
  Knowing that, he decided he would view his work as a career,
  not some job he took just to pay the bills.

- *If you don't believe in your company, why should anyone
  else?* If you can't look a prospective customer in the eye and

confidently tell them you believe you're their best option, why would they ever place their business with you? No company is perfect and sometimes you have to acknowledge a competitor might be the right choice. That kind of integrity will win you more business than you lose.

- *The customer isn't always right and that's why they need a good salesperson.* This one shocked John because it went against the old adage that the customer was always right. Then he realized, how can anyone always be right? Especially in the absence of all the information? A prospective customer will never know as much about your company, your products and services, or competitors as a good salesperson. This understanding can be used to gently show prospects there might be a better way than they're currently considering.

- *"Selling is the process of persuading a person that your product or service is of greater value to him or her than the price you're asking for it."* John heard this quote from sales guru Brian Tracy used several times in the sales training. It made sense because it reminded him of what he'd learned about the science of influence in that psych class during his freshman year of college. Persuasion was the underpinning of selling.

- *People prefer to do business with people they like.* This also took him back to that psych class. He remembered his likability was a big reason he got the job offers. He was beginning to realize what he learned in the class was the secret for dealing with people and selling.

- *"Yes!" is critical for your professional success and personal happiness.* John knew success in sales was contingent on getting customers to say yes. He also saw that getting to yes was critical to get the company to adopt any new ideas he might come up with. On a personal level he knew he'd never get a date without hearing yes first.

While John learned much more during the first two months of training, these pearls of wisdom stood out from the rest.

Shadowing

The two months of in-house training seemed to fly by for all the trainees. Just as John had been ready for college to end, he was ready for this learning to conclude. It wasn't that he was bored; his head hurt from all the new knowledge he'd crammed into it over the eight weeks! Beyond that, he was excited to spend the next month shadowing different sales reps. Each was unique so he knew he would glean a variety of new perspectives.

Ben was the old timer of the bunch. He'd been in the industry for 25 years and joined the company when it started. Not only had he seen a lot when it came to technology changes in health care, nobody knew the company like he did.

Francesca wasn't much older than John. She had joined the company straight out of college and was doing great. John felt he could learn a lot from her because she was successfully walking the path he was about to start on, just a little further down the road.

Russell was in his early 30s, originally from Pittsburgh, he made the move to North Carolina when he started with MediTech. John heard Russell had an uncanny ability to size up people quickly, so he was eager to learn Russell's secrets.

Rich was in his early 40s. He'd been with more than a half dozen companies during his career and joined MediTech three years before John. He had a reputation as a "natural born salesman."

The last rep John would spend a week with was Nancy. She was in her late 30s and was very efficient with her time. That came out of necessity because she balanced her career with marriage and raising two young boys.

Making Friends with Ben

Ben Blackstone was in his late 40s and reminded John of his dad. Ben was like Todd in that most issues were black and white, right or wrong, good or bad. John would silently chuckle when Ben would routinely make statements like, "There are two kinds of people in the world: those who are your customers and those who aren't," and, "When I was your age…"

Ben had a very laid-back way about him when it came to his sales calls. His casual approach reminded John of a golfer who didn't try to kill the ball but who swung easy and always landed the shot in the middle of the fairway. Those golfers made the game look effortless, and Ben did the same with sales. For Ben, a sales call was just a conversation between friends. That was evident because John could see how much Ben's customers liked him.

On their third day together, as they drove down a lonely country road in Ben's company car, John finally worked up the courage to ask Ben about his relationships. "Ben, something I've noticed is how much your customers like you. What do you do to get them to like you?"

Ben, eyes focused on the road ahead, casually replied, "I don't do anything to get them to like me."

John pressed him, "You must do something to get them to like you as much as they do."

"Nope, I never try to get a customer to like me," Ben answered with a slight grin.

John, getting a little frustrated, said, "Okay, I give up. Clearly I'm missing something. What's your secret?"

Ben's eyes lit up and he said, "John, I'm glad you asked. Most people who ask the questions you asked think I'm pulling their leg and stop short of finding out the secret to great relationships."

John furrowed his brow and inquired, "So what's the secret Ben?"

"The secret is…" Ben paused to build the anticipation, then went on, "I do my darndest to like my customers."

Staring at Ben, somewhat confused, John asked, "I don't get it Ben. I know you like them but why do they like you?"

Ben elaborated, "John, once people know you truly like them, it's almost impossible not to like you in return. But your liking must be genuine. People have BS meters and can detect insincerity a mile away."

John leaned in, "But what do you do to like them?"

Ben got straight to the point, "I take two simple approaches to like people. First, I make every effort to find out what we have in common. I do that because it's natural for people to like other people they see as similar to themselves. Have you ever met someone who cheered for your favorite football team, and you found you instantly liked them?"

"All the time," John quickly replied. "Anybody who cheers for my team is okay in my book."

"Exactly! See, it's not about them liking you, it's about you connecting on something you have in common so you'll like them. My second approach is to pay people compliments when warranted. People don't offer compliments nearly enough so when you do, that kind act is like giving a tall glass of water to a thirsty person – they drink it up!" Ben said with what was now becoming a familiar grin.

"But what if the person is kind of a jerk?" John interjected.

Ben responded enthusiastically, "Great question! Abraham Lincoln once said, *'I don't like that man. I must get to know him better.'* I believe honest Abe and I'm a firm believer there's good in everyone. With some people you have to look a little harder but when you find a good quality then pay a genuine compliment, you'll be amazed at the difference it makes. Difficult people seldom get compliments so they're dying from thirst but don't seem to realize it. When you give them that cool glass of water, they appreciate it much more than most people!"

"Ben, you make it sound so simple," John noted.

Wrapping up the conversation as they pulled into the parking lot for their next appointment Ben said, "That's because it is simple John. *Always have this mindset with whomever you meet: 'I want to like this person.' Then connect and compliment.* The more you do it, the easier it gets until it's just naturally who you are."

John threw Ben's great pearl of wisdom onto a sticky note: *Don't try to get people to like you. Instead, come to like other people.* This reminded him of the liking principle he first encountered in college, but Ben's advice took it to a whole new level. It also alerted him to something he had mistakenly done. He spent so much effort on getting people to like him that he realized now he might have come across as desperate to make friends. He vowed to start making an effort to like everyone he met.

Superstar Francesca

Next up was Francesca Martinez. If John could get a nugget of wisdom from Francesca like he did from Ben, he knew it would be another great week. John was impressed with Francesca because, despite youth and lack of experience compared to other reps, she was in the top 10% of all salespeople in just her second full year with the company. This intrigued John so he wanted to find out what she attributed her success to.

They met in the cafeteria at the headquarters for a quick cup of coffee on Monday morning before hitting the road for sales calls. John started the conversation with a genuine compliment and question, "Francesca, I'm sure you know this but I'll say it anyway, you have a great reputation in the company. I know you're one of the top salespeople in just your second year and people refer to you as a superstar. What do you believe is the reason for your success?"

Francesca started by giving credit to Ben. "John, I owe a lot to Ben. Everything started slowly that first year. When he told me to like my customers, and I put his advice into practice, it kickstarted opportunities. I noticed people became more willing to have sales calls and were also willing to give me extra time. I really sensed they enjoyed having me around."

"Ben told me about that. So that's all I need to do?" John asked.

"No, there's much more to it for younger reps like you and me. What Ben taught me was only the door opener. Beyond that I needed people to have confidence in me and whatever I was sharing," Francesca added.

"How can you do that when you have so little experience to lean on?" John inquired.

"When customers are unsure what to do, we need to help them overcome that uncertainty. I discovered a few ways to make that happen. First, I asked my boss to re-introduce me to customers. I sensed there were facts they didn't know about me that, if they knew, might make them pay more attention."

"What did the letter say?" John asked.

Francesca told John, "Toastmasters taught me the value of a third-party introduction. Think about the times you've listened to a speaker at a conference. Before he or she speaks, someone introduces the speaker to the audience. Good speakers leave nothing to chance so they write their own intros so the audience knows their credentials. A third party can make statements that, if the speaker shared firsthand, might sound like they were bragging. Understanding this, I wrote the letter for my boss."

Curious, John asked, "What did it say?"

Francesca anticipated the question and said, "I thought you might ask so I brought a copy along for you." John looked at the letter and read the following:

Dr. Sutton,

I know you've met Francesca Martinez on a couple of occasions, but I was remiss in not formally introducing her when we assigned her as your sales rep. Francesca is an impressive individual but not one to toot her own horn. I on the other hand don't mind doing that on behalf of her.

Francesca joined us just over a year ago after graduating magna cum laude from Emory University. We interviewed more than a dozen people for the position she now occupies and she was easily our top choice.

During the second half of her first year she was already in the top quartile of our salespeople. That's because she's dedicated herself to understanding our company, our products, and most importantly, her clients. She's poured herself into learning all she can and it shows based on the feedback I've received from her clients.

In addition to her work, Francesca has become an active member of our community. She's involved in Rotary and takes one week each summer to volunteer at a camp for kids.

I hope you enjoy working with Francesca as much as we enjoy having her on our team.

Cathy Metcalf
Vice President, Sales & Marketing

Smiling, John looked up and said, "Well done Francesca. I didn't know all of that about you. I was already impressed with you but now even more so!"

Francesca replied, "Thank you John. The email helped me get more appointments for sure. But there's something else that's just as important. It's great to be set up as some kind of expert but then you have to back it up when you open your mouth."

John asked, "How do you do that?"

Francesca shared, "*To present yourself as an expert go beyond your credentials. Always cite your sources.* This is especially important for newer reps like you and I because we're still building our expertise. When you don't cite sources, what you share might come across as merely an opinion. However, when you say, 'According to the New England Journal of Medicine...' or quote notable experts, people pay more attention."

Looking down at her watch she said, "We can continue this conversation in the car. We need to get going because I always like to be ten minutes early for appointments." With that they headed out the door for their first sales call.

John was amazed at how his mind kept going back to what he learned in the Psych 101 class. This time he connected Francesca's advice with the principle of authority. What he took away from Francesca was: *Become an expert in your field then make sure people know about your expertise.* This meant he had a lot to learn about the business and he needed to think about how he would like to be introduced when he got his new territory.

Understanding People with Russell

John was excited to meet with Russell Frazier and continue his learning. Russell's background was different from John's, and it went beyond race. John had not spent much time in big cities, but Russell grew up in one of the larger cities in the country. John knew Russell's perspective had to be different from his and most people John grew up with. Also, because of Russell's reputation for understanding people, John felt time with him would add another arrow to his quiver of knowledge.

The first few days with Russell were different from those with Ben and Francesca. For starters, Russell was less talkative. Gradually John began to notice it was because he asked a lot of questions then let John do most of the talking. That wasn't bad because John was comfortable talking about himself and his family.

Something else that stood out about Russell was that he seemed to be more perceptive of everything and everyone around him. John could tell that based on what Russell commented about and because of the questions he asked.

It was during a quick stop for lunch at McDonald's that John inquired about it. Munching on a Big Mac, Russell told John he grew up in what most people would consider a tough neighborhood in Pittsburgh. He said, "Where I came from, to avoid trouble I had to be aware of my surroundings and I learned to size up people quickly." Finally, this was the opening John was hoping for. It matched Russell's reputation for understanding people.

John quickly asked Russell, "Can you tell me how you took what you learned growing up in Pittsburgh and translated it into understanding customers?"

Setting down his burger and looking directly at John, Russell shared, "At first it was hard. Others saw something in me, this ability to figure out people that they didn't possess. It wasn't something I formally learned, it just kind of happened. It was part of who I was which made it difficult to explain to people let alone try to teach them what I knew."

After taking a sip of his Diet Coke John went on, "You said 'at first.' Does that mean now it's different?"

Russell responded, almost pointing a French fry at John, "Good catch. You see, you're already getting the hang of it."

"What do you mean?" John asked.

"I came to realize the reason I was able to figure out people came down to three habits. First, I'm curious. I ask good questions that will get others to reveal bits and pieces of who they are. Second, I listen. I pay close attention to what people say and the words they use. Words reveal a lot about what people believe and how they view the world. Finally, I pay attention to what their bodies and faces are telling me." Russell went on, "John, you asked a good question then caught something most people would miss. You noticed I said, 'at first' then asked me how it's different now."

"I honestly didn't know I was doing that," John confessed as he finished the last of his fries.

Russell encouraged him, "Perhaps it's hit or miss right now, as it was for me, but if you take what I'm sharing with you, begin to focus on it and practice, soon it will become second nature for you. That's the essence of learning."

John went on, "I get the good questions and listening but what did you mean when you mentioned bodies and faces?"

"Growing up where I did, there were plenty of people who would lie to your face. Unfortunately, there are people in business who will do the same too. If you pay attention to their facial expressions and body language, you'll do a much better job determining whether or not they're telling you the truth. There's no one expression or body movement that gives them away but you begin to put everything together so you can make a good determination. If you don't think you're getting the straight scoop, keep asking questions. When people aren't telling you the truth they'll eventually slip up."

"Wow, that's fascinating. I have to say, growing up where I did, I pretty much took everyone at face value. My mom used to say I was too trusting," John shared. He went on, "I never really understood what she meant but after hearing you, I'm starting to understand."

Russell had something else to share as they gathered their trays and dumped their trash into the bins near the door. He stopped by the door, turned to John and said, "Here's a big tell about people's character: Do they do what they say they will? Most people do this because they don't want to feel bad about themselves and don't want to look bad in front of others. To figure this out, don't tell people what to do, ask them instead. That way they'll say yes or no. For example, I often ask clients, 'If we can make the changes you say your clients need, will you place your next order with us?' If they say yes, I learn a lot about them by whether or not they follow through on their word."

As they got in the car John thanked Russell, not only for what he learned but because Russell was candid about his upbringing. That helped John understand why he was so good when it came to understanding people. The first takeaway was *Ask, don't tell, to gain a commitment and learn about character.* Once again John realized he'd heard this before. He recalled reading about the principle of consistency in *Influence: The Psychology of Persuasion*.

John also wrote down, *Ask good questions then listen with your eyes and ears.* This made so much sense but was never something he consciously focused on.

Rich the Stereotypical Salesman

Almost immediately John was a little uneasy when he met with Rich Bennett. He couldn't put his finger on it at first because Rich was nice enough, outgoing, and very gregarious. His customers seemed to like him initially because he brought a certain energy and flair to his sales calls. That's what earned him the reputation as a natural born salesman, but something didn't add up for John. What he experienced was quite a different feeling than he had during his time with Ben, Francesca, and Russell.

Rich went by Flick, a humorous and memorable nickname from his childhood. The nickname was appropriate because he always had his sunglasses on, talked non-stop, and seemed to have a joke ready for any situation. However, even at his young age and with his lack of business experience, John sensed the jokes were sometimes inappropriate. Clients sheepishly laughed at Flick's humor but there was an uneasiness about it, like they knew their laughter only encouraged him.

When they drove from one sales call to another Flick would go on and on about his career, often badmouthing prior employers and bosses. That didn't sit well with John. No one seemed to know as much about anything, especially sales, as Flick thought he knew.

"John, I'm gonna give you some career advice most people think but never say out loud," Flick said as they drove along an open stretch of highway. "Don't stay in one place too long. I've never been with any employer for more than four years."

Curious, not so much about the advice but rather, to gain insight into Flick, John asked, "Why do you say that?"

Looking straight ahead with his head bobbing side to side as if he didn't have a care in the world, Flick continued, "Two reasons. First, no employer will be loyal to you so there's no need for you to feel loyalty to them. Second, the grass is always greener somewhere else because there's always someone else willing to pay you a little more."

John was enjoying everything about MediTech so far, especially the people, but Flick seemed like an outlier so he wasn't sure how to respond. He thought maybe the issue was Flick's lack of loyalty, not the companies he'd worked for. Because Flick seemed to blurt out whatever he was thinking John said, "I appreciate you sharing that. I know you've been here for three years already so are you looking for your next opportunity?"

Flick said somewhat smugly, "Usually the opportunities find me but yeah, I'm always keeping my eyes open for the next big thing." Flick continued talking but it was too much for John and his thoughts began to wander. He occasionally nodded his head or grunted a reply to act as if he was interested in what Flick was sharing. After a while he could tell Flick was talking more to hear himself than anything else so John stopped pretending and just enjoyed the scenery as they took some backroads through small North Carolina towns.

The more sales calls they made the more John heard Flick's banter with clients. He felt like he was watching the much-despised hard sell sales approach. It was manipulative because Flick would say or do anything to make the sale. Whatever a client asked, Flick claimed the company could do or would do. This caught John's attention because, having just spent two months learning about MediTech's products and services, he knew Flick was often stretching the truth and sometimes outright lying.

Fortunately, John only had to spend two days with Flick. By the end of their time together John started to wonder if Flick's career, moving from company to company, was more like a criminal staying one step ahead of the law. He talked a good game then moved on to the next opportunity before he was found out.

Flick was everything people dislike about stereotypical salespeople and John was disappointed that he had to spend precious time with him during training. However, the more he thought about those couple of days, the more he saw it had been a great learning opportunity. When he thought back to coaches or teachers he didn't respect he realized *he learned what not to do or how not to act from each*. That was the case with Flick – if you want to succeed in business, here's what not to do. He summed it up this way, *"Don't be a Flick."*

Nancy's Balancing Act

Nancy Elders was last in the rotation of people John would shadow. He looked forward to his three days with her because one day he hoped to get married and have a family. Thinking about time with Nancy made him realize the sooner he got a handle on how to balance work, family, and personal interests the better off he would be. He related it back to something he picked up playing sports: learning good skills and habits early always paid dividends over the long haul.

Nancy was waiting for John each day in front of the office precisely at 8:00 a.m. and he was dropped off promptly at 4:30 each afternoon. Nancy maintained her schedule with the kids and work in a way that would make the toughest Marine proud. Her obligations outside of work left little extra time to devote to her career. This meant there was no time wasted as she squeezed everything she could out of every minute of each day. John didn't say anything, but he was a little intimidated by her initially.

As soon as John's bottom hit the car seat they were off. Nancy filled him in on each client as they drove from appointment to appointment. He wondered how she could know so much given that she had little time outside of normal work hours. She let John know that she took a memory course to help her with that. She learned to chunk information in ways that made it easier to remember. John asked if she could explain what chunking was.

Nancy shared the following with John, "If I asked you to name all the furniture in your house you might struggle a bit. But, if I asked you about the furniture in your living room you could easily tell me about each piece. Then we'd move to the kitchen followed by the dining room. If we hit every room, you would remember so much more because you can visualize the furniture in each room. That's basically what chunking is: put what you know into categories that will be easy to remember. I couldn't possibly recall all the physicians I interact with at a large hospital but when I chunk them by specialty such as orthopedics, cardiology, or infectious disease, it's easy. Get it?"

"That's so simple but brilliant," John exclaimed.

She went on, "I look for every shortcut I can because they make me more efficient. I know I can accomplish more in eight hours than most of my peers do in 10 or more hours. Work smarter, not longer."

"Makes sense," John acknowledged. Then he asked, "What would you say is the biggest key to maintaining a healthy balance between your family, work, and whatever outside interests you have?"

"That goes back to something I did just before we had children. I worked a lot more hours back then. My husband's job required him to travel quite often and still does. I didn't want to give up my career but with my territory being local we agreed I would be the primary caregiver for the kids. It was around that time that a friend gave me a copy of Steven Covey's book, *The 7 Habits of Highly Effective People*. There was a chapter called 'Begin with the End in Mind' where Covey encouraged readers to write a personal mission statement. It made sense to me because every business I've ever worked for had a written mission statement. I took inventory of my life and what I wanted to be remembered for when it was all said and done. I looked at my faith, family, personal interests, and my career."

"That's inspiring. Can you tell me a little bit about your mission statement?" John asked.

Nancy replied, "Without going into details I will say this: I chose to prioritize my faith first, family second, myself as an individual, then my career. I love what I do but I make daily choices to not let my career overshadow my faith, family, or personal well-being. At times in my career that meant getting passed over for opportunities, but

I was able to accept those decisions because I was living life on my terms. That's freedom and it's one of the best feelings you can have."

She went on to ask, "John, have you ever considered writing a mission statement?"

John confessed, "I haven't because I'd never heard of a mission statement until now. But, based on what you've shared, I'm going to pick up that book and think about writing one."

Nancy was blunt when she said, "John, during my career I've encountered more people than I care to acknowledge who had good intentions but didn't follow through on activities that would benefit them so I'm going to be very direct and ask you: will you commit to writing a personal mission statement within the next six months?"

How could he say no? Before he realized it, he heard himself say, "Yes, I will write one." Thinking about Russell and what he said about commitments he knew he was on the hook with Nancy. She ended the conversation telling John she was going to follow up in six months if she didn't hear from him first.

As John reflected on his time with Nancy he realized she had treated him like the teachers and coaches he enjoyed most. She was demanding something from him that was in his best interest. He knew her time was precious and the fact that she would take some of that time to follow up with him added weight to the commitment. The takeaway with Nancy was, *Think about who you are and who you want to be then write a mission statement for accountability.* He knew this exercise would take time, effort, and a lot of thought.

Now the Work Begins

Graduation Again

The big day finally arrived for John and the other new associates. They were graduating from trainee status to full-fledged MediTech sales reps. That meant a bump in pay, new titles, and territory assignments. Although John was a Midwest kid, he was game to go anywhere.

The company treated the whole placement process as a special event because they knew there were certain times in life where celebrations made a big difference. High school and college graduations, weddings, certain birthdays, and milestone anniversaries, were just a few examples. Not only was MediTech's graduation ceremony special, but it also bonded the group together and created even more loyalty to the company. The cohesive training experience had been very good for everyone, and they understood the company had made a big investment in them.

When it came time for assignments the company treated it like the NFL and NBA drafts. There were balloons and banners hanging from the walls and ceiling of the training auditorium. In addition to the senior executives who were in town that day, Ben, Francesca, Russell, and Nancy all attended the event which meant a lot to John and the other trainees. Flick on the other hand was noticeably absent.

Cathy Metcalf, the Vice President of Sales & Marketing, oversaw the MediTech draft. In round two she looked at the audience and said, "With their pick the Southwest Region chooses John Andrews!" There was applause as he rose from his seat and walked to the podium to stand next to Cathy. The Southwest territory included Texas, New Mexico, and Arizona, so John got to choose which hat he wanted to put on: Texas Longhorns, New Mexico Lobos, or Arizona State Sun Devils. He chose the Longhorns ball cap.

John would move out West to work with Duane Edwards. Like Ben, Duane was a long timer in the medical supply industry. He'd done extremely well during his career and retired early as one of the top sales reps for the second largest company in the industry. However, Cathy was able to talk him out of retirement about five years ago when MediTech decided to open the Southwest Region. Duane trained Cathy early in her career and felt invested in her, so he naturally wanted to help when she came calling. Besides that, he missed being in the game.

Memories fade quickly and Duane had forgotten how hard opening a new territory was. While far from the biggest in the company, the region had the potential to become the largest in time because of the movement of retirees from all over the country to the warm, dry climate of the Southwest. He was looking forward to working with John and investing in him as he'd done with Cathy because he was a coach at heart. Likewise, John eagerly anticipated learning all he could from Duane as he slowly took the reins from him.

The Move

John was asked to move to Dallas, at least for the first year, so he would be close to Duane while they worked together. After that he could live anywhere in the three-state region. Dallas was more than okay with John because he knew the weather was much nicer than where he'd grown up in the Midwest and it was a vibrant city with lots of activities for young, single people. The icing on the cake was he could get anywhere quickly flying out of the DFW Airport or Love Field.

John was excited when he made his first trip to Dallas to scout out apartments that fall. Duane pulled up curbside at the airport in his big Lincoln Continental to welcome John to Texas. John knew Duane would be there but had no idea his wife Sally would be joining him. They reminded John of his parents which made him feel at home in an unfamiliar place. They insisted he stay with them rather than in some nearby hotel because, as Duane told him, there would be more hotel nights than he could count in the coming years.

When Duane asked John what he wanted in an apartment John mentioned being close to Duane, easy access to the airport, and hopefully a place where there were other young professionals. Much to his surprise, Duane scouted out half a dozen places to visit over the next few days. Ironically, several were places John was considering from doing his own research.

When John and Duane started driving to the first apartment complex John thanked him for all he'd done in such a short time. He started, "Duane, I want to say thanks for how you and Sally have extended yourselves for me. You didn't have to do anything and I would have been fine. Having me stay with you, then Sally's breakfast this morning, is such a nice way to start this trip."

Duane replied, "John, first of all, you're welcome. I don't do what I do for thanks, but it always means a lot when someone recognizes the little things and appreciates the effort."

John said, "What you and Sally have done is not little. It might seem like it to you but it's huge in my eyes. On top of picking me up and staying with you, the fact that you heard what I said about an apartment and got a list blew me away. I did my own research and found some places I wanted to look at. Four of the six you shared were on my list. That gives me confidence that we're on the same page and that they're good places."

As they made their way onto the highway Duane told John, "I had someone who invested in me early in my career and I never forgot how it made me feel and how much it helped. I've come to realize that being a giver and helping people has several benefits. First, it feels good and it's a chance to replicate the best parts of ourselves. I hope that doesn't sound selfish."

"Not at all," John replied.

The highway was crowded and traffic was moving slowly. As they eased along Duane went on, "Second, it makes the other person feel good. Two people feeling good is a win-win. And that leads to the third benefit. The people you help along the way are the people who will be most willing to help you when you need it. But let me caution you John – don't help people just to get their help. If people think you're only helping to get something in return they'll probably reject your offers. Make sense?"

"Absolutely," John replied, remembering his early mistake in college of asking to borrow his friend's car right after helping that friend with his term paper. John went on, "This is how I translate it: *Don't give to get, but if you don't give, you'll never get.*"

"Bingo!" Duane exclaimed. "You're a fast learner John. I'm looking forward to our time together."

"Duane, I've already learned so much from everyone I've spent time with. As I start putting together what I'm learning I feel like I'm assembling a puzzle. I don't know what the picture is yet, but I know there's a picture." John shared.

"That's an interesting way to look at it John," Duane replied.

"Can I take a moment to share how I see a couple of the puzzle pieces fitting together already?" John asked.

"I'm intrigued. Go for it!" Duane encouraged him.

John went on, "During my time with Ben I learned *one key to building relationships is making the choice to like the people you meet.*"

Duane responded, "That's great advice Ben gave you."

John continued, "What occurs to me is, *the more I do that the more I'll genuinely want to help people.* It's natural to want to help your friends so the more I look at people like you and Sally, our current and future customers, or anyone else I meet, and see them as friends the more genuine my giving will be. It all but removes 'give to get' or manipulation from the relationship equation. Does that make sense?"

By this point they were in the parking lot for their first apartment visit. Just before getting out of the car Duane turned to John, eyes wide, and replied, "Wow, that's profound John. I never looked at it that way but it makes total sense. It moves what you're learning from good advice to a philosophy to live by. And I thought I'd be the one doing the teaching. Now I'm even more excited about our time together!"

Before John went to bed that night he wrote down what he learned that day. Giving was the heart of reciprocity. He recalled from his reading that people feel obligated to give back to those who first give to them. He summarized it as follows: *Don't give to get, but if you don't give, you'll never get.*

Even more profound was his insight about the connection between liking and reciprocity. Here's what he wrote: *Truly liking the people I interact with will make my giving more genuine because I naturally want to help my friends.*

Duane the Sales Coach

With Duane and Sally's help John found a nice two-bedroom town-house apartment about 15 minutes from their place. The apartment complex was only five years old, had a large pool, a two-story party house, and most residents were in their mid 20s and early 30s. After a short trip home to pack up his belongings and say goodbye to his family, John settled into Dallas in early November.

His time with Duane reminded him of the weeks shadowing the sales reps, only more hands-on. Not surprisingly, Flick had left the company, but Ben, Francesca, Russell, and Nancy remained. John considered each a friend and mentor. Duane however was definitely a coach. Some people use the terms mentor and coach interchangeably but they're different and that didn't escape John's notice.

Mentors were people John knew he could rely on for advice and guidance. Depending on the situation he went to different people. For example, if he had a relationship building question Ben was his man. If he wanted to understand people, especially customers, he knew Russell was the best person to talk with. Likewise, for practical advice navigating his new career Francesca was his go to person because she'd walked the path he was on. Nancy was his straight shooter for issues of efficiency and work-life balance.

Spending time with Duane helped him see how a coach was different from a mentor. As a coach Duane was getting ready to entrust John with the territory he'd come out of retirement to build. Duane knew he was responsible for John's professional growth and ultimately his production. Mentors had no stake in the game if John didn't perform well but Duane did. He wanted to know his customers would be well cared for and that the territory he'd invested so much time and effort in would continue to grow once he retired. *Duane described his coaching as follows: The process of improving performance and results through timely feedback.*

Duane knew if John focused on the right skills and habits (performance) the results would take care of themselves. If the results weren't there, then they'd go back to the drawing board to see if they were working on the right skills and activities. In addition to teaching, a big part of Duane's role was to give John timely feedback so he could course correct when necessary and continually try new approaches.

Being a true Texan, Duane told John, "My grandfather drove a stagecoach. Until the advent of the automobile, the stagecoach was the best way to get from one place to another. As your coach, I'm responsible for helping you get from where you are to where you need to be so you're ready to take over the Southwest Region."

Duane was a savvy coach and knew if he just told John what to do he wouldn't "own it" like he would if he came up with an idea himself. That's why Duane always asked John what he thought the right course of action might be. Even if he wasn't in total agreement, he'd give John the opportunity to try it his way. Afterwards they'd debrief and more questions would follow.

When they traveled together they took one of three approaches to their sales calls:

- On demonstration calls Duane would conduct the sales call, demonstrating the behaviors needed to have a successful meeting, while John watched and took notes.
- Joint calls were meetings with customers where Duane and John each had predetermined roles.
- During observation calls Duane let John take the lead then observed John's performance.

Early on most calls were demonstration calls. Gradually they worked into joint calls and after about seven months most were observation sales calls with John steering the ship. Whatever approach they went with, immediately after the call, usually in the car on the way to their next appointment, they talked about whether or not they thought it was a successful sales call. That was followed by what went well, what could have been better, and what they might try differently next time.

Something John learned for the first time was what it meant to go on a sales call. He thought any time you went to see a customer it was a sales call, but he soon learned that was incorrect. Duane never talked about visiting customers. He said "visits" were reserved for friends and family because there were no business expectations. Sales calls were different because there were expectations around business from both parties. He told John a sales call had one of three goals:

1. Leave with new business in hand,
2. Get a commitment for future business, or
3. Know what must change to start getting business.

It's not that there weren't opportunities to go on relationship building calls. There were times when they wanted to meet new employees of their customers, celebrate milestones, or just take clients to lunch or dinner as a way of saying thanks for their business. However, Duane said he'd seen too many sales reps default to relationship calls because they were easy, fun, and didn't risk rejection. Duane believed if a sales rep helped clients solve problems that would make for happy, satisfied customers.

John was soaking everything up like a sponge. He had several take-aways he knew would serve him well during his career. The first was what it meant to go on a sales call. He wrote: *Sales calls involve getting business, obtaining commitments for business, or agreeing on next steps to start generating business.* That was simple and straightforward.

His other learning point was: *If we can help people solve problems, we'll have happy, satisfied customers.* He realized it wasn't rocket science but was starting to see how so many salespeople miss these fundamentals.

Life Outside of Work

John's time in Dallas wasn't all work and no play. He used his week-nights to explore the city. He started making friends at a local gym he joined shortly after settling into his apartment. He'd run on and off over the years with his involvement in sports, so he decided to get in 5K races on weekends. He reasoned it would be another way to meet people and give him the chance to see new parts of the state. He spent weekends in Austin, San Antonio, Houston, and El Paso because of races and started making friends.

He'd taken Nancy's idea about a mission statement and run with it, pun intended. After reading Steven Covey's *The 7 Habits of Highly Effective People,* John began work on his mission statement. Writing it was harder than he anticipated because there was a lot to consider when thinking about the potential scope of his life and how he'd like to be remembered. To gain a wider perspective he talked with his parents, siblings, a couple of friends, and Duane, who was becoming more than just a coach for John.

Just as he was finishing his mission statement, he was thrown a curveball. He'd been so focused on work and running that dating wasn't something he pursued. That changed one day in January when he met Abigail at the gym. A pretty brunette in her early 20s, he'd seen her before but usually she was on her way out when he was arriving. On this day they ended up on treadmills next to each other. It was a perfect opportunity to start a conversation. For a moment his mind was flooded with anxiety and his palms became sweaty as thoughts about his high school dating experiences popped up. Then suddenly Ben's advice came to mind – like the people you meet. A little enamored by Abigail's big green eyes and pretty smile, he didn't think it would be too hard to find reasons to like her.

He tried to play it cool while he was warming up on the treadmill and casually said, "I've seen you here before, but it always seems like you're leaving when I arrive. Why are you in late today?"

"Long day at work," she replied, not indicating there would be any further conversation.

Not deterred he went on, "I get it. I'm new to Dallas. I just started a new job." Then he asked a non-threatening question, "What do you do?"

Abigail said, "I work for a physician's group at a local hospital. I'm a nurse."

"Really?" John said with a hint of surprise in his voice. Remembering how having things in common with people can build rapport through the principle of liking he shared, "I'm in health care too. I work for MediTech Supplies."

That caught Abigail's attention and she told John, "I've heard of you guys. In fact, I think one of your reps, Duane somebody, talked with one of our physicians some time ago."

"Crazy coincidence, Duane is training me. I'll be taking over his territory when he retires at the end of the year."

"I don't believe in coincidence. If everything that happened in my life was just coincidence then I should fall to my knees and worship coincidence," Abigail said with a smile as she looked at John.

Not wanting to miss an opportunity, he mustered up his courage and replied, "Well if it's not coincidence, we should continue this conversation over coffee sometime so we can find out what it is."

"Wow, that's bold! I like confident people. Sure, we can do that. I'll be done in 45 minutes. There's a small coffee shop at the end of the mall we can walk to," Abigail suggested as she flashed a smile at John.

Truthfully, John wasn't expecting that response and, although it meant cutting his workout short, he decided to jump at the chance to spend time with her. Trying hard to still act casual and conceal his excitement he said, "Sold! I'll meet you at the front desk in 45."

Coincidence, or perhaps fate, that day on the treadmills was the start of a relationship for John and Abigail. Abigail was from Dallas, so she was able to introduce John to more people and take him to fun places. In addition to their focus on fitness, John enjoyed the fact that each understood what the other did and the challenges they faced in their careers.

More than ever, John was seeing that all the philosophies, principles, and skills he was learning on the job applied just as much to his personal life. Nowhere was this clearer than in his relationship with Abigail, especially when the time came to meet her family a few months into their relationship. Just as he focused on getting to know his customers, understanding their needs, and paying close attention with his eyes and ears, he used these same skills with Abigail, her parents, and siblings. It wasn't that he was faking it or using some sales technique. On the contrary, John was internalizing the ethical principles of influence and slowly but surely influence was becoming natural and unforced. The time with Abigail and her family confirmed something he'd written a while ago: *"Yes!" is critical for professional success and personal happiness.* Getting Abigail to say yes to coffee that day in the gym certainly added to his personal happiness.

The relationship with Abigail had him rethink parts of his mission statement because he could envision spending his life with her. Almost six months to the date after he spoke with Nancy, he finalized his mission statement and sent it to her.

Nancy,

I hope all is well with you and your family. It was nearly six months ago that we spent time together and you asked if I was going to write a personal mission statement. I committed to that and have enclosed what I wrote.

I thought I'd have it to you sooner, but I met someone who caused me to rethink parts of it. Her name is Abigail and I hope you get to meet her someday. The conversation you and I had, as well as seeing how you balanced family and work, had a tremendous impact on my thinking. Thank you!

I look forward to seeing you at the next sales meeting.

Sincerely,
John

Below is what John sent to Nancy.

Mission: When my time on earth is over, I want people to say about my life, "Well done!" In pursuit of this I will focus on my spiritual growth, my family, myself as an individual, and my career.

Spiritual: I want my relationship with God to be the priority in my life. I will love my neighbor as myself and remember it's better to give than receive.

Family: I will make my family my priority second only to my relationship with God. I will love and honor my wife and children. I will meet their needs to the best of my ability and help them live happy, fulfilled lives by giving unconditional love. I want to earn my family's respect and be the kind of husband and father they can be proud of.

Personal: I will maintain a balance between my mental and physical health; live my life with integrity; be open to change and accept when I'm wrong; be a good listener; continue to develop in the areas of loving, learning, and relationships. I need to remember that I have free will and a choice in all matters. I will seek to understand others before trying to be understood. I will strive to be the best I can be at whatever I do.

Career: I hope to be remembered for making my workplace better for having been there in a productive and personal sense. I will put forth my best effort to whatever task is given to me. I will focus on helping others. I want to obtain satisfaction from my career; be fair and honest while remaining firm and decisive; always remember the people involved; earn the trust, respect, and confidence of those I work with; continue to develop professionally and seek new challenges.

Conclusion: I work to live; I don't live to work. I will never sacrifice my spiritual, personal, or family's well-being at the expense of my career.

When Nancy read John's mission statement it made her day. It's always exciting to see someone take advice and put it into practice because all too often helpful advice falls on deaf ears. She knew John's mission statement would serve him well as his career unfolded so she sent him a congratulatory note to let him know that.

Taking Over

Surprised by the Timing

John was about to experience another milestone. He'd been working with Duane for 10 months and had been in the driver's seat, taking the lead on most sales calls, the last several months. Duane surprised John one afternoon while they were in Phoenix to see clients. After leaving their final appointment for the day Duane told John he was ready to take the reins full time.

"John, you're ready to take over," he casually said on the drive back to the hotel.

"What? Are you sure Duane?" John replied with a bit of a stutter. "I feel like I still have so much to learn. Besides, we're supposed to work together until the end of the year." He realized how much it still meant to have Duane with him even if he was taking the lead on sales calls. His mind went back to when he learned to drive. There was a noticeable difference the first few times he drove without his mom, dad, or anyone else in the car. There was a comfort level when someone was with him in the car and the same feeling applied to Duane coming along on sales calls.

Duane stressed this didn't mean that he wouldn't be available to John. "I promised Cathy I'd devote myself to you until the end of the year and I'm going to keep my word. But you've progressed so rapidly that I can let you take over and we'll just consult whenever you need me. I've enjoyed my time with you John so the offer to help extends beyond my retirement at the end of the year. I'm invested in you and your success."

John didn't know what to say. He was overwhelmed. It wasn't so much taking over as it was how grateful he was to Duane and how much he meant to him as a coach and friend. He said, "Duane, I could never repay you for your kindness and willingness to share your wisdom with me. I felt more like family than a coworker. I know how hard you worked to get the Southwest Region up and running. I promise I will grow it into something that will make you proud."

With a smile that radiated confidence Duane said, "John, I know you will. It's my baby and I'm giving it to you to raise from this point forward. I appreciate you acknowledging the time and effort I've put into you and our time together. Now I'm going to ask for a favor."

"Whatever you want Duane," John quickly interjected.

"Will you pay it forward John?" Duane asked as he looked John in the eye.

"Absolutely!" John said without hesitation.

"John, when we started working together I told you someone invested in me early in my career. I never forgot how much it meant and how much it helped me. Investing in others feels good and you get to replicate the best parts of yourself. In addition, it makes the other person feel valued and they'll want to help you when you need it."

"Duane, I remember you saying that when we first met. It would be an honor to impact people in the same way that you've impacted my life. It goes way beyond work," John told him. The sincerity in John's voice meant a lot to Duane.

The next step was to inform Cathy about the accelerated plan. Duane proposed to Cathy that they make a joint announcement about Duane's impending retirement and inform customers that John would take over the Southwest Region immediately. She agreed it was a good plan.

Recalling what he'd learned about the need for a strong introduction to build authority, John asked if he could write the section about himself for the announcement. It was an easy sell with Duane once he shared the logic behind his request. Cathy was on board too because she'd done that with other reps and was aware of how it helped set them up for success. Cathy's announcement read as follows:

It's with a mixture of sadness and joy that I'm reaching out to you today to let you know Duane Edwards will retire at year-end. Duane came out of retirement five years ago because of our professional relationship and deep friendship. MediTech Supplies wanted to open operations in the Southwest and I could think of no one better than Duane to help us.

I cannot overstate how much I owe to Duane. He trained me when I started in the business then helped me when I needed it most. I'm proud I began my career with him and that I'm here for him as he closes out his career.

As you know, Duane has taken John Andrews under his wing, sharing everything he knows with John. Duane told me, "The Southwest Region and our customers are my baby and now I'm giving my baby to John to raise."

John came on board with us just over a year ago. Seldom have I seen a young person come into this business with as much excitement and desire to learn as John has. He hasn't done everything we've asked of him...he's done so much more!

Because you've dealt with Duane for many years, I hope you'll not look at John as a new rep but as Duane's hand-picked successor. Duane and I have confidence in John's ability to do great things for you, your organization, and the clients you serve. We hope you share that confidence.

With thanks and gratitude,
Cathy Metcalf
Vice President, Sales & Marketing

As John reflected on everything that was taking place he was a bit overwhelmed. He knew this was inevitable, but it was happening so fast. He didn't want to lose another opportunity for growth. As he thought about what he'd learned from Duane beyond just business he wrote the following:

Pay it forward: Giving is an investment in others that will pay dividends for them and you.

It's okay to feel good when you help others. Humans will naturally do what feels good, so this is a reinforcement mechanism.

Delayed Flights

John's relationship with Abigail was getting more serious. She was excited for him as he prepared to take over for Duane. Before his first solo trip she took him to dinner to celebrate and surprised John by inviting her parents to join them. She wanted to make it a special night for him.

They met at Pasquale's, a small, family owned, Italian restaurant in a trendy neighborhood on the outskirts of Dallas. It looked like a hole in the wall but had a reputation as having the best lasagna and pizza in the metro area.

Abigail's father was a marketing manager for a large publishing company and knew taking ownership of sales for an entire region was a big career step. After his toast and well wishes they had a delightful evening.

It was Monday morning and John arrived at the airport a few hours before his scheduled flight to Phoenix. He had a late afternoon meeting planned then dinner with another client. Shortly after arriving he noticed flight delays popping up on the board. Apparently there were storms in the Midwest that were delaying flights out of St. Louis, Chicago, Detroit, and other major airports. Before long he saw his flight was delayed by two hours. That meant no afternoon meeting and, if it were delayed any further, dinner would have to be scrapped.

Unfortunately, he would not be able to reschedule either appointment because the next three days were packed with client meetings and dinners.

He decided he should see what options were available, so he got in line at the ticket counter. He'd not been flying long enough to feel the frustration that frequent travelers were experiencing so he was a bit surprised by many reactions. Most travelers let their frustration get the best of them and they became very demanding with the airline employees. "You don't understand. I have to be there by 2:00 p.m.!" one traveler practically shouted.

John felt bad for the airline employees because he rightly understood the weather was out of their control. By the time he got to the counter customer service reps were noticeably frustrated and it was seeping out towards the travelers. Everyone was on edge so he paused and thought about what he could do. He recalled Ben's sage advice, "Like the people you meet. Everyone has some good in them. Find the good and pay a genuine compliment."

He asked Colleen, the ticketing agent, "I don't travel too much. Does this happen often?"

She was taken back by the question and said, "Doesn't matter how often it happens. Whenever it does, it ruins everyone's day."

"Sorry to hear that. I've been watching the interactions and feel bad for all of you. I know you can't control the weather and you're doing the best you can," he said in an empathetic tone.

Colleen looked him in the eye and said, "Thank you. I really appreciate that. I wish more travelers would acknowledge what you just shared. How can I help you?"

"I'm scheduled to go to Phoenix in a couple of hours. I have an afternoon meeting and dinner. If I make them that would be great, but if not, I'm sure my clients will understand. What are my options?" John asked.

Feeling less stressed and able to think more clearly, Colleen began looking for options. She didn't mind doing a little extra work for kind people. "Mr. Andrews, I appreciate your understanding of the situation. I see we have an open seat on a flight that leaves in 30 minutes. I can get you on that flight, but your checked bag won't make it to Phoenix till late afternoon or early evening. If you're okay with that I can make the switch."

"That would be awesome. I can do without the bag if I can make my client meetings. Thank you so much!" he said to her.

Colleen smiled, feeling good about making a customer happy in the midst of all the chaos. As she worked on changing the reservation and printing the ticket she asked John, "Do you go to Phoenix much?"

"With my job I'll be going there at least once a month," he said.

"Tell you what; I'm usually at this gate most days. If you need any travel help, come find me and I'll take care of you," she told him.

"Thanks Colleen. It will be nice to see a friendly face when I come to the airport," he said as he grabbed his ticket and headed to his new departure gate.

Here were more valuable lessons: *Don't react to situations, make the choice to respond.* He recognized reacting based on emotion, as most passengers were doing, usually inflamed stressful situations, and worked against them. Matching negative emotions in stressful situations was like pouring gas on a fire hoping to put it out.

"Look for the good and pay a genuine compliment if you want to make a friend," went from good advice to a practical reality because he made a new friend with Colleen, someone who would prove to be very helpful in the near future. He decided to take the compliment a step further and sent an email to the airlines to let them know what a good job Colleen had done during a stressful situation. While he was still in Phoenix he received an email from the airline in reply to his note:

Dear Mr. Andrews,
We value your business and appreciate that you took time to tell us about your experience with Colleen a few days ago. We strive to provide the kind of service that will keep customers happy and wanting to fly with us.

It is apparent Colleen did just that. When we learn about employees who delight customers, we make sure to recognize them. In Colleen's case we shared the email you wrote and will reward her with an extra day off with pay.

Again, thank you for taking the time to recognize Colleen. It meant a lot to her and to us.

Sincerely,
Kim Floyd
Vice President, Customer Service

The Intimidating Client

Thanks to Colleen's assistance John was able to make it to Phoenix on time. He was especially pleased because his afternoon meeting was with MediTech's largest client in the state, and he would be meeting with the lead physician in the practice.

John met Dr. Michaels briefly while traveling with Duane shortly after arriving in Texas. He remembered Dr. Michaels had been practicing medicine since before John was born. John knew that because the doctor reminded him of that fact more than once. Dr. Michaels was well respected by his staff but came across as all business because he was so precise about everything. John naturally assumed that was because, being a heart surgeon, he couldn't afford any slip ups.

John spoke to Abigail just before leaving for the appointment with Dr. Michaels. He wanted her to know that despite the weather he was able to get to Phoenix on time. More than that, he wanted to talk with her to get a boost of confidence. He briefly shared a little about the first time he met Dr. Michaels and confided to Abigail that he was nervous. He'd been with MediTech for just over a year and was about to meet with a man who'd been practicing medicine for nearly four decades. To make matters more difficult, he was meeting at the doctor's office.

Despite the background noise in the office Abigail listened intently. When John finally paused, she spoke up and asked if she could give John a bit of advice. When he agreed she said in a reassuring tone, "John, don't try to fake anything because he'll see right through it. I've always found I gain people's trust when I'm honest about my shortcomings."

Still nervous, John replied, "If I admit weakness he'll run roughshod over me."

"John, I've been working with doctors for a few years and can tell you, they're human just like you and me. They may be very smart, but their brains are no different than ours. If you're honest about how you're feeling, you'll be perceived as genuine and that goes a long way. Trust me on this," she continued in her reassuring way.

How could John not trust her? He remembered a story from his vacation Bible school days as a child. It was about King David meeting a woman named Abigail who became one of his wives. She was described as beautiful, virtuous, and wise. That described Abigail to a tee, so he decided to trust her wisdom.

He arrived a few minutes early but was kept waiting for 15 minutes. Rather than assume Dr. Michaels was playing a game he focused on what he wanted to say to kick off the meeting. Finally, he was told he could see the doctor and was escorted to his office.

The office had an air of prestige about it. The big desk was mahogany and the plush carpet was hunter green. The bookcases were lined with medical journals as well as biographies of famous people throughout history. On the walls were Dr. Michaels' degrees, awards, and various certificates of achievement. It was quite intimidating for John until he reflected back to Abigail's advice. He took a deep breath and opened the meeting saying, "Dr. Michaels, nice to see you again. You may recall we met last fall when I accompanied Duane on sales calls."

"I do remember you. How could I forget, you reminded me of one of my grandsons," he said with a slight grin. John took it as a reminder of his age and inexperience.

"Well, I hope you'll enjoy me coming around as much as you enjoy seeing your grandson," John shot back with a confident smile. Before Dr. Michaels could say anything, John continued, "Dr. Michaels, I want to be upfront with you. Of all my sales calls this week, this is the only one I'm nervous about. That's because I know you see me as young and not having the experience Duane possessed. But I bring a few qualities to the table I think you'll appreciate. First is excitement. Do you remember how excited you were when you started out?"

"I may be old, but you never forget certain times in life. Yes, I remember the youthful excitement coming out of medical school," Dr. Michaels said with a wide grin as he thought about practicing medicine after graduation. He went on, "John, hazing the newbie comes with the territory. And you're right about me looking at your inexperience. But I'm also wise enough to know you bring tech savvy to the table. I can hardly keep up with all the changes taking place. That's where you can provide value for me; keep me informed on the latest technology that can help me and my partners give our patients the best care possible. You do that and we'll see where this goes. Does that sound fair?"

John could barely contain his excitement, "I can absolutely do that. I promise you this, no medical supply rep will do a better job when it comes to keeping you informed than I will."

"Then we're going to get along just fine," Dr. Michaels said.

The rest of the meeting went smoothly as John shared a few new MediTech products, told Dr. Michaels what was coming down the pike, and answered his numerous questions. All of John's nerves were gone by the time the meeting concluded and they shook hands.

As John drove his rental car back to the hotel, he reflected on two learning points. First was the decision to call Abigail. He felt closer to her for having trusted her enough to share his feelings. He was beginning to see her as an important part of his success.

The second reflection, which he wrote down, was, *admit a weakness or shortcoming to gain trust.* He recalled hearing that in the psych class when he learned about the principle of authority. But, like so much he learned, it was a distant memory until he saw the real-world application. He recognized Dr. Michaels saw him as self-aware and honest because of the way he started the meeting. John also realized it wasn't enough to admit weakness and leave it there because he didn't want others to simply focus on his shortcomings. *The key to leveraging this psychology was transitioning away from his weaknesses with words like "but" or "however" into his strengths.* That's exactly what he'd done when he owned up to his nerves but then talked about his excitement.

Unexpected News

John arrived home late Thursday night from his first solo business trip. He was on a cloud because he couldn't have imagined the trip going any better. He told Abigail he wanted to take her out for dinner to celebrate. It was late afternoon on Saturday when he started getting ready for the evening and his phone rang. Thinking it was Abigail, he picked up the phone but instantly realized it was his mom. As soon as he heard her voice he could tell something was wrong.

"Johnny," she said fighting back tears, "something terrible has happened. Your father had a stroke. He's in the hospital. Can you come home?"

"Of course I can Mom. How bad is it?" he asked with a concerned tone.

"We don't know yet. He can't talk and the doctors are running tests. Carey and Billy are on their way home," she said.

At that moment John realized he'd never known his mom to be scared. She was always the voice of reason, the calm person when things were turbulent, the person who looked for the positive in every situation. He reassured her, "Mom, as soon as we hang up I'll catch the first flight I can."

When he hung up he called Abigail to let her know what happened and that he was heading home. She asked if she could accompany him, even if it was just for a few days.

He knew this would not be an ideal way to introduce her to his family, but he wanted her support. And, because Abigail was a nurse, he thought that might help the family interpret the doctor's messages. He agreed and told her he would swing by her place to pick her up within the hour.

Next, he called Duane to let him know what was going on. Duane told John to get him his agenda for next week along with his sales call notes. Duane said he would call each client over the weekend to let them know he would be there in John's place.

As John reflected on Abigail's offer to drop everything to accompany him and Duane's willingness to jump in without hesitation, he realized how blessed he was to have them both in his life.

John and Abigail arrived at the airport and who did they see but Colleen.

Colleen said, "John, are you heading back to Arizona already?"

"No, I'm heading home. Family emergency. My mom called a few hours ago and said my dad had a stroke," John shared, not thinking how little he knew Colleen to share something so personal.

"I'm so sorry to hear that," Colleen replied with an empathetic tone.

A little flustered John said, "Colleen, this is my girlfriend Abigail. She's traveling home with me."

"Nice to meet you Abigail. I'm sorry it has to be under these circumstances," Colleen said. At that moment all of Colleen's customer experience training kicked in as she asked John in a calm, reassuring voice, "What flight are you on?"

He shared the flight number and she quickly keyed in the flight into the computer. A moment later a smile came across Colleen's face and she informed John and Abigail that she'd just moved them up to first class. John tried to object but she insisted, saying they didn't need any more stress. They thanked Colleen, grabbed their tickets, and waited patiently to board their flight.

"She was so nice John. She acted like she's known you for quite some time," Abigail said, trying to make small talk to distract John.

"I actually met her earlier this week," John replied as he recounted the story of the delayed flights and his conversation with Colleen.

Abigail was drawn to John even more after hearing the story. She said, "Being a nurse, I've seen the worst come out in people during stressful times. The fact that you carried yourself so well that you made a friend says a lot about your character."

John said he'd heard a quote from Aristotle that stuck with him, *"Character may almost be called the most effective means of persuasion."* He went on to tell Abigail he was learning that more than anything, people respond to others not because of what they know or what they have but because of who they are. That's what happened with Colleen.

By the time their flight landed it was just after midnight. Billy met them as soon as they made their way to the baggage claim area. He was glad to see John because he'd not seen him since Christmas. He was surprised to see John holding hands with an unfamiliar young lady.

After a bear hug typical of brothers, John introduced Billy to Abigail. "Billy, this is Abigail. We've been dating since the beginning of the year. When I told her what happened to Dad she said she wanted to come with me. In addition to support, she's a nurse and might help us with questions for the doctors."

"Very nice to meet you Abigail. Thanks for being there for John and our family," Billy said as they grabbed their luggage and made their way to the parking garage.

Before they knew it, they were walking into John's childhood home. His mom was still up, waiting for him and Billy to get home, just like she did when they were teenagers. After a long embrace John introduced his mother to Abigail. Jane immediately hugged her and treated Abigail as if she'd been a part of the family for years. As she showed Abigail to the guest room they talked about how Abigail and John met. It was well past 2:00 a.m. before everyone finally fell asleep.

John and Abigail woke up to the smell of bacon because Carey was making breakfast. She'd arrived earlier the day before and had been asleep when they came in. It was yet another introduction for Abigail but by now she was getting used to it. Because of her easy, outgoing personality, big green eyes, and a captivating smile everyone instantly fell in love with her. She felt very at home with John's family because they were down to earth just like her family.

Soon enough it would be visiting hours, so they headed to the hospital to get an update on Todd. As they entered the building it was apparent Abigail felt comfortable in the medical setting and before they knew it she had them in the waiting area outside of Todd's room. Once she informed the nurse behind the desk that she too was a nurse it was easy to persuade him to page the attending physician right away.

The doctor arrived within minutes and told the family that Todd had a restful night. In a very matter of fact voice she said, "Todd's heart, weight, and other vitals are good so I'm surprised he would suffer a stroke at his age. We'll need to run more tests to try to determine the cause." After answering some questions she informed them that, depending on Todd's progress, he might be into rehab within a week. She told Jane if the stroke was stress related Todd might need to consider early retirement.

All of this was good news considering what could have been. As the family talked about the future Abigail spent more time with the doctor. She gathered as much detail as possible and asked questions that might never occur to Jane or anyone else.

Before John and Abigail headed back to Dallas they'd received good news. Todd was expected to make a full recovery, but the doctor did recommend early retirement out of an abundance of caution. This was about five years sooner than expected but between Todd's planning and the reassurances of Billy, Carey, and John to help however they could, Jane knew they'd be fine.

The Next Phase

Much Needed Advice

As the doctor anticipated, Todd made a full recovery. At first he resisted the idea of retiring but relented based on the advice of the doctor and the concern the family showed. To occupy his time he began to focus on his health and hobbies. One old hobby he picked up was photography and he soon found that he was pretty good at it. After a few people asked him to do photos for them he decided to turn the pastime into a small business to supplement his retirement income.

Knowing his dad was on the road to recovery, John devoted his attention and efforts to his career and his relationship with Abigail. His relationship with Duane went from coach to friend and mentor. There wasn't a week that went by where they didn't speak for at least half an hour. Every month Sally insisted John and Abigail join her and Duane for dinner.

At work, John's territory was growing faster than expected so Cathy Metcalf was thrilled. John attributed his success to what Duane taught him, but Duane assured John that he was taking everything to new heights by thoughtfully putting into practice all that he was learning.

Despite his success John was restless and he knew exactly why. After dating for more than a year he was ready to make his relationship with Abigail permanent. They'd spoken about marriage on several occasions but as he thought about popping the question he found himself nervous in a way he'd not felt before, not even early on with dating. He thought about discussing it with Duane but decided this was something he needed to talk over with his dad.

After thinking about it all week John finally worked up the courage to make the call on Sunday afternoon. Pacing the floor, he dialed the phone. "Dad, it's John," he said after his dad picked up the phone.

"What's up Johnny?" Todd asked with a smile in his voice.

Todd's positive, upbeat tone caught John's attention. His dad used to be a lot more serious and reserved. "Dad, you sound happy and relaxed."

"Johnny, I've never been happier. The stroke was a wakeup call. I was so focused on work that I was missing out on a lot of life. None of us is guaranteed tomorrow so I made a promise to your mom that I wasn't going to let another day slip by without expressing gratitude and joy."

John almost couldn't believe what he was hearing. He joked, "Excuse me but could you put my dad on the phone?"

Todd laughed, "Touché son. So, what's up?"

"Well dad, I called because I wanted to talk with you about the next big decision I have to make."

Todd remembered their talk about the job offer years ago and assumed John might be considering a career move. He was surprised when he heard John say, "I want to ask Abigail to marry me but I'm not sure how to go about it. I've never been so nervous about anything in my life."

"Wow Johnny, I thought you were going to ask about work," Todd replied with surprise in his voice.

John nervously went on, "How did you ask mom to marry you?"

"Well, we'd gone through a rough patch," Todd began. "I was indecisive, so we were on and off for a few months. When I finally settled things in my heart, I knew I had some ground to make up. The first step was to ask her father for her hand in marriage. That was rough. He was hard on me because he'd seen her cry a few times when we weren't going out. He said I took his grilling like a man and that's what gave him the confidence to say yes to me."

"But what about Mom, how did you ask her?" John inquired.

"Because I had some making up to do, I knew I couldn't just ask her out of the blue. I decided to go all out with flowers, wine, a romantic dinner downtown, and a horse drawn carriage ride. It was during the carriage ride that I popped the question. She said it was like a fairy tale and there was no way she could say no."

John quickly thought about another piece of psychology that he'd learned about, pre-suasion. He remembered it was all about setting the stage, that doing certain things in advance of making your ask could make it easier for someone to say yes.

"Dad, you're a genius!" John said.

"I think a lot of people would dispute that, but I appreciate the compliment. I take it that's what you were looking for?" he asked John.

"Yes, it's the advice I needed." Just before he got off the phone he said, "Thanks Dad, I love you."

Todd had a smile on his face and a tear in his eye as he hung up. He was able to fully enjoy the moment, something that had eluded him in the past.

As he'd done so many times before, John stopped everything he was doing so he could write down what he'd learned during that conversation.

Tomorrow isn't guaranteed so enjoy every day. That tapped into scarcity, the feeling of wanting something more when you know it's limited. We think we'll live forever until we're confronted with the truth that we won't. John was determined to keep this one front and center.

He knew if he tapped into pre-suasion by giving more thought to setting the stage before important moments that yes would come sooner and more often.

A Pre-suasive Proposal

John took his dad's advice and contacted Abigail's father, Pete, without her knowing it. He asked Pete if they could meet for a drink because he had something important to talk about. Like Todd, Pete assumed John might be looking for some career advice and gladly accepted.

They met at Joe's Bar and Grill near the house where Abigail grew up. The bar was exactly what you'd expect from a place called Joe's, a neighborhood joint where the locals went, and everyone knew each other. The drinks were inexpensive and the burgers tasted like they were cooked over a backyard grill using real charcoal. And of course, the bartender was Joe, the owner.

John arrived early so he could rehearse in his mind how the conversation might go. Pete arrived right on time and noticed John was a little fidgety. As they began to talk he became acutely aware that John was uncharacteristically stumbling over his words, so he said, "John, is there something you want to ask me?"

John started off with, "Yes sir," He hadn't called Pete sir since the very first day they met. He went on, "I love your daughter. The first thing I noticed was her beauty when I saw her at the gym. But as I got to know her I saw she was more beautiful on the inside. I can't see myself without her."

Pete quickly discerned what was taking place and, enjoying the moment, decided to string it out. John was normally so composed that it was fun to see him a little uncomfortable for a change. He said, "I get it John. Abigail has been a joy for us to raise. I can't see life without her either."

"Then you know what I'm getting at," John replied.

"No, I'm not sure I do John. Is there something more?" Pete said, trying to conceal a grin as he glanced up at the ballgame on the big screen television.

"Well, actually there is. I'd like…"

"Another drink?" Pete asked, cutting him off, as he finished his beer.

"No. I'd like your permission to marry Abigail," John finally blurted out.

"Oh, is that all?" Pete said as he started to laugh. "John, you're a fine young man. Abigail's mother and I have enjoyed getting to know you and we'd be honored to have Abigail marry you...if she wants to."

"If she wants to?" John asked with a concerned look on his face and tone in his voice.

"Relax John, I'm pulling your leg. She loves you so I have no doubt what she'll say," Pete said with a chuckle.

With that John sighed a sense of relief. He'd not realized how nervous he was until that moment. It was like watching a scary movie in the theater but not knowing how tense you were until the movie was over and you were walking out of the theater with all the other moviegoers. John finally relaxed and they enjoyed the rest of their time together.

Saturday, April 26th was the big day. John had it all mapped out, a day of activities Abigail enjoyed most. He knew a fun filled day together would set the stage for a memorable proposal. It started with him picking her up for coffee that morning. She loved going to coffee shops and talking. It reminded her of when she was a little girl and her dad would take her to different coffee shops and bookstores. She always felt like an adult on those father-daughter dates. The fact that John and Abigail's first date took place over coffee made it special for them too.

Next they were off to the zoo. Again, a favorite activity for Abigail because of the childhood memories. As they walked around the zoo exhibits they talked about how they met that day on the treadmills at the gym. An outsider might have brushed it off as a random event, their timing on that day, but they both agreed it wasn't a coincidence.

John expressed how much it meant to him and his family that she was there during his dad's stroke. It wasn't an ideal way for her to meet everyone but when people go through deep emotional experiences those tend to be bonding moments. He let her know how much his family loved her. She returned the sentiment for his family and talked about how her parents liked him more than anyone else she'd dated.

As they made their way around the zoo the monkeys and apes caught their attention, especially how the mothers dealt with the babies. That led to a natural conversation about kids; how many did each want, if they had some what they would look like, what would they name them, and so on.

John said he was having such a nice day that he didn't want it to end. He asked if they could go to dinner. Of course, this was part of the plan too. He'd made a reservation at a rooftop restaurant because it was going to be a full moon, something else he knew Abigail loved, as signified by the crescent moon tattoo on her right wrist.

The evening was going as planned then it came time for dessert. Abigail said no thanks to more food, but John insisted she try just one bite of the house specialty. He'd arranged with the staff to have the engagement ring under a covered dish which was supposed to be the dessert tray. When it came out John built it up as some exotic treat that she would never forget. As he lifted the lid off the tray the diamond ring sparkled in the moonlight. Abigail was breathless as John dropped to a knee and said, "Abigail, no long speech. I just want you to know I love you and want this day to last forever in your memory. Will you marry me?"

With tears in her eyes she joked, "I thought you were going to ask me in front of the gorilla cage. This is so much better. Yes!" At that moment they both heard the wait staff and diners cheer and clap.

His relationship with Abigail was so strong he probably didn't need to pre-suade her but he knew his efforts would make the day special, something they would tell their children and grandchildren about.

Six months later, in late October, they were married in front of family, friends, and a small host of people from MediTech. John was surprised and delighted that Dr. Michaels flew in from Phoenix. After their initial meeting the relationship turned a corner and, true to his promise, John was keeping Dr. Michaels abreast of new technologies.

Apparently Dr. Michaels was serious when he told John he reminded him of his grandson.

John and Abigail spent a week in Hawaii for their honeymoon. Abigail thought she knew John but was continually amazed as she watched him interact with airline employees, hotel staff, restaurant servers, store owners, and complete strangers. *It seemed as if John always got what he asked for and left people happier for having helped him.* She realized she needed to learn his secrets.

How to DEAL with People

Just prior to the wedding they found a small apartment that would suit their needs. It was smaller than either of their prior places, but they decided to downsize to save as much money as they could for a house. His dad's planning had rubbed off on John.

One day, as John and Abigail were arranging furniture in the apartment, Abigail broached the subject of John's interactions with people.

"John, when I first met you I saw your confidence on the treadmill when you asked me out. I was impressed. As I've watched you since then, especially during our honeymoon, something has caught my attention."

Not knowing what she was referring to, John tentatively asked, "What's that?"

Abigail went on, "You have this Zen-like ability to not only get people to do what you want but to be happy about doing it. What's your secret?"

"If I told you then you'd use it on me," he said with a laugh.

Abigail shot back, "If you don't tell me I might have to walk out that door. Isn't that what you call scarcity?" She smiled, then went on, "Seriously, working with rational doctors and emotional patients every day is tough on me. It's hard to go from one extreme to another immediately. Anything I can do to make it easier I want to learn."

Abigail had been such an important person for John that he looked forward to sharing with her all that he was learning. "Abigail, I'd be happy to help you." He took her back to college and talked about the Psych 101 class where he first encountered the science of influence. He told her about the principles he learned and how they came to life as he started his career.

He said he was noticing certain personalities responded better to specific principles. Then he started telling her about people with the *driver personality.*

"Probably the toughest person for me to deal with is a driver. That's someone who is very focused on getting tasks done with little regard for relationships. They also like to be in control of the situations they find themselves in," he shared.

He went on, "Initially I made the mistake of focusing too much on relationship building. It was a mistake because drivers just don't care too much about making friends. *What I've found to be most effective with drivers are three approaches: consistency, authority, and scarcity.* When drivers say or do something, they believe they're right because of extreme confidence, or sometimes big egos. If I can tap back into what they've said or done it makes it much easier to get them to see what I'm trying to share. That's consistency. Next is authority. They want data, sources, and information from credible people. Last but not least is scarcity. Drivers hate to lose! I honestly point out what they might miss out on by not going along with my proposal and it's easier to win them over. Does all that make sense?"

"That makes total sense," Abigail said. Many doctors she knew were off the chart drivers and she could see these approaches would help her quite a bit. "What's next?" she asked.

"*Expressive people* are like drivers in that they want to be in control. However, they differ because they are relationship people. Getting work done takes a back seat to getting to know people so these folks were much easier for me to deal with," John shared. He continued, "*To influence expressives I look to use liking, reciprocity, and social proof.* Because they're relationship driven, I tap into liking. I do all

I can to get to know them and let them get to know me. Next, I look for opportunities to help them anyway I can. That's reciprocity and it's also a relationship builder. When I give, these people are the people most willing to help me when I need it. Finally, I engage social proof by sharing what others are doing. With a focus on relationships, expressives care a lot about what other people are saying, what they're doing, and how they're feeling."

"Oh my gosh," Abigail exclaimed, "that's brilliant." She was envisioning some of the executives at the hospital as John talked. These were people who needed to put on events and raise money. She would have called them back slappers or glad handers prior to John's description but now she knew better.

"Should I continue?" John asked as they moved a couch from the corner of the room to the center to see how it would look.

"Only if you want to stay married," she joked while putting the pillows on the couch.

"Alright, next are *amiable types*. These are relationship-oriented people who are not controlling but focus more on self-control. *I've found using liking, social proof, and authority work best with amiables.* I engage the principle of liking by focusing on what we have in common and paying genuine compliments. Because these people are relationship driven this means quite a bit. I find amiables are generally laid back and willing to go with the flow so I use social proof to let them know how others think and feel about whatever I'm sharing. Finally, comes authority. I was surprised by this one, but amiable people respond to information and individuals in higher up positions."

Abigail chimed in, "The description reminds me of a lot of nurses. We do respond to information and sometimes have a hard time challenging a doctor's authority. All the nurses I know appreciate authentic people and recognition. And yes, we do care about what others are doing. This is so helpful!"

"Okay, here's the last personality I look for, *the logical person*. These individuals focus on tasks but don't care about controlling others or situations. They're a little more inwardly focused and rule oriented.

Knowing this, *look to employ authority, consistency, and reciprocity with logical people.* Authority is a no brainer, for them it's all about sources of information and data. When they think through a problem and come to a conclusion they do so because of intellect, not ego. When I circle back to their prior decisions or actions, I'm engaging the psychology of consistency and they tend to go along with what I propose. If you're like me then reciprocity might surprise you. But the more I thought about it the more sense it made. Reciprocity is a rule all human societies operate by and logicals are rule oriented people. They may not comply or help out of the goodness of their hearts but rather a need to follow the rule," he concluded.

"I can see this with some doctors and administrators," Abigail told John. "I'm excited to start trying this approach at work. I know people respond to me because I'm nice but that doesn't always work so I feel better equipped to deal with people now."

"Abigail, you may not have caught it but *take the first letter from Driver, Expressive, Amiable, and Logical and you get the acronym DEAL. I've found it an easy way to remember all four personalities because we DEAL with people every day,*" John said with a wink and a smile.

By the end of the conversation they'd finished rearranging the living room. Rather than tackling another room right away they ordered pizza and decided to watch a movie to relax.

Family Practice

In January John made a trip to New Mexico. Not nearly as populous as Arizona or Texas, he didn't have many clients in the state so he was looking for prospects in Albuquerque and Santa Fe. That's where he met Al Harris, the lead physician in an unusual medical facility. Upon arriving at the newly furnished office John felt different than he did with other clients. He noticed a deep camaraderie among the employees. Everyone was friendly, not only with clients, but each other. It went beyond smiles and greetings; they seemed to genuinely enjoy helping each other. It was a family practice that seemed like it was run by an actual family.

After spending time touring the facility they moved to Al's office. While he was in Al's office John listened with his eyes and ears. What he noticed was unmistakable.

John took Al to lunch so they could relax and get to know one another. "Al, I do my best to pay close attention to people and the environments I'm in. Something stood out about your office," John started out.

"Oh really," Al replied after swallowing a bite of his salad. "What's that?"

Setting down his fork, John went on, "There's a closeness between your staff, almost like family. It's unlike anything I've noticed in other physician's practices. What do you attribute it to?"

Wiping his mouth with the cloth napkin, looking straight into John's eyes, Al said, "John, I'm going to share something with you that I don't tell most people unless I see a need for help or the curiosity you displayed. I'm a recovering alcoholic."

John was taken back because he never would have imagined someone as outgoing, friendly, and successful as Al would struggle with alcohol. Apparently his face betrayed his thoughts because Al said, "You look surprised John."

A little embarrassed, looking down rather than directly at Al, John confessed, "Al, you don't fit the image I had of an alcoholic. I mean, recovering alcoholic."

Al laughed and that put John at ease. "Don't worry John, you're not alone in that thought. We come in all shapes, sizes, backgrounds, and walks of life. I've been sober for 30 years now."

"Congratulations! But what does all of this have to do with what I noticed in the office?" John inquired.

"Not only am I alcoholic," Al said, "Nearly everyone who works for me is on the road to recovery." He smiled as he shared that, proud that he was able to help people who are sometimes marginalized by employers.

That blew John away. Curious he went on, "I had no idea and never would have guessed. I don't know anyone who is an alcoholic so I wonder; how can you trust someone who struggles with alcohol?"

"Usually when I invite someone in for an interview they feel unqualified to work in an office environment like ours. I tell them if they can beat the disease then anything we ask them to do will seem easy by comparison. They usually light up, as if they're thinking, 'I never thought of that, but he might be right!'"

John asked an obvious question, "What do you do when someone relapses?"

Finishing his salad, Al said, "We love 'em, support 'em, and get them the help they need. If they get back on track, we take 'em back. If they don't, we let them know we're still here to support them, but we need people we can rely on because our patients count on us. We've only lost two people in 20 years."

"That's incredible Al. How does that tie into the family atmosphere I sensed?" John inquired as he sipped his iced tea.

"Family is as close as we can get. Helping family members is almost like helping ourselves because we share the same genes. The depth of the relationship between alcoholics isn't genetic but it's almost unparalleled. Perhaps only people who've served in the military share as close a bond. I think most alcoholics would agree with me when I say helping another alcoholic is almost like helping myself and when they help me, they're also helping themselves. Does that make sense?" Al asked John.

"Completely," John replied. "I think it goes to something I learned in college. There is a psychological principle called unity that describes it. That principle says *it's easier for people to say yes to those they see as one of them, part of the tribe, so to speak.* I've always noticed the 'band of brothers' with the military but now I see it can apply to people and groups I never considered before."

Al shared, "I know what we're doing is good and it works so well because we're all in the same boat. It can be tough on regular businesses to hire alcoholics just as it might be for some ex-military to assimilate into ordinary life. There's a brotherhood in each case that helps."

"Al, I appreciate your authenticity and trust to share all of this with me, especially since this is the first time we've met. I really look forward to learning more from you as we continue to get to know each other," John said as he got ready to sign the credit card slip.

When he went back to the hotel he quickly wrote what he learned from Al. Unity was a concept John understood in his head but not in his heart...until that day with Al. He wrote, *"Unity is about shared identity. People will be most likely to help others with whom they share an identity. It's almost as if we is me and me is we."*

Everything is New

House Hunting

After more than a year in their tiny apartment John and Abigail decided they were ready to start looking for a home. No matter how much two people love each other, and no matter how cozy, a 900 square foot apartment doesn't afford much personal space when needed. More importantly, their future plans included children so the sooner they found the right place the better off they thought they'd be. They certainly didn't want to try moving if Abigail happened to get pregnant.

Mandy, one of Abigail's good friends going back to grade school, told her a house just went on the market in her neighborhood. Although they didn't have a realtor, John and Abigail decided to look at the house because they'd been to Mandy's place and liked the family friendly atmosphere of the neighborhood.

It was a very middle-class neighborhood for Texas. Most of the brick homes were only 25-30 years old, the trees lining the streets were mature, and the yards were spacious. You didn't have to spend much time there to see there were lots of kids. A big plus was the elementary school that was within walking distance. It seemed like an ideal place to possibly start their family.

They walked into the home and were greeted by Joe, the realtor. He was in his early sixties, had a big belly and a bigger smile. John whispered to Abigail, "He reminds me of Santa Claus," which made her smile. Seeing them, Joe's smile grew wider despite not knowing what they were talking about. They couldn't help but like him right away.

The four bedroom home stood out in the neighborhood because it was white stucco. The black trim around the windows and doors, plus some black wrought iron, accentuated the home's features. There were dozens of red, yellow, and white flowers of various types in front of the little stone fence in the front yard.

Although they loved the house and thought it would be nice to live close to Mandy, they felt there was no way they could buy the first house they looked at. Who does that? And besides, most couples have a hard time agreeing on the details of such a monumental under-taking. They thought they were caught up in the excitement of see-ing that first house and imagining themselves as homeowners. John approached Joe and said, "Joe, we really like this place but there's no way we could buy the first home we looked at. I'm sure you under-stand. But I do have some good news for you."

Without a hint of disappointment Joe asked, "And what's that?"

John continued, "We don't have a realtor yet so we were wondering if you'd like to be our representative and show us some other places in the immediate area?"

With an ever-widening smile Joe exclaimed, "I'd be happy to take you and Abigail on as clients. I do want to let you know some-thing about this place before we start looking at others. This was a showcase home in the Parade of Homes 25 years ago. There's only one other like it in the neighborhood...and I live in it. I tell you that because it's a wonderful neighborhood." That one state-ment instantly caused John to trust Joe. It was no different than knowing a car salesman drove the same car you were considering buying. If it's good enough for the salesman, then it's probably a good car.

After a couple of weeks looking at different neighborhoods in town and adjacent ones Abigail turned to John, "I have to be honest, the house I like most is the place in Mandy's neighborhood where we met

Joe. I know it seems weird to think we might buy the first house we looked at, but I can't get it out of my mind."

"I'm glad you said that because I was feeling the same way," John started. "And I like the fact that you'd be so close to a good friend, especially with me traveling so much."

Negotiating with Joe was easy because they liked and trusted him. The feeling was mutual, Joe thought the world of John and Abigail even though he'd only known them for a short time. He'd been in real estate for several decades and felt he was a good judge of character, so he was excited at the prospect of having another nice young couple coming into his neighborhood.

While a buyer would always like to pay as little as possible and a seller would like to get as much as possible, each side made a few concessions until they hit the point where they were in agreement. *As Joe so aptly put it, "When it comes to negotiating a deal ethically, I believe in this axiom: Good for you, good for me, then we're good to go!"* That saying struck a chord with John so he jotted it down. He believed when you get beyond all the negotiating tactics what's most important is that each party trusts the other. *For John, trust was knowing each party was truthful. That is, not only did they tell the truth, they didn't hide the truth either.* For example, if there had been a crack in the basement floor and Joe had not told them, it wouldn't be defensible to say, "You didn't ask." The fact that Joe did point out a few defects in the house showed he was interested in making a fair and honest sale.

Between their jobs and savings, getting the necessary financing was no problem for John and Abigail. Before they knew it, they were signing a bevy of papers and were officially homeowners, strapped to a 30-year mortgage.

A New Neighbor

When John and Abigail made the move from their apartment into their first home they were greeted by Larry as they unloaded the rental truck. Larry had lived in the neighborhood for nearly 20 years and was affectionately called Bud by everyone who knew him. That's because he quickly became everyone's buddy. He lived in the house immediately to the right of John and Abigail's place as you faced their home.

Bud had been an insurance rep for a large company for nearly 40 years and retired a few years before John and Abigail moved into the neighborhood. He loved life and was always up for a party. The later the party went, the deeper the conversation would go with Bud. Life, death, faith, and social justice were topics he had fun engaging over. Not even sex, politics, or religion were off limits for Bud. If you didn't know him you might be taken aback by some of his questions. However, if you knew him you knew he was harmless, the questions were out of curiosity, and you loved the man.

The first few months he was always there for John and Abigail. Whatever they needed – a tool, yard items, recommendations for home repairs – Bud had it or knew where to get it. John and Abigail appreciated him because they had no idea about all the items you needed when you transitioned from an apartment to a home.

It wasn't just the new couple Bud helped, he offered assistance to anyone in the neighborhood. John noticed Bud seemed happiest when the neighbors were happy. That was a rare quality so he decided to ask Bud about it one hot summer day. It was Saturday afternoon and each finished cutting the grass around the same time. As they cleaned up John walked across the backyard with a couple of beers in hand and offered one to Bud. Never wanting to offend a neighbor...or turn away a free beer...Bud graciously accepted.

Wiping his brow John said, "Bud, Abigail and I cannot tell you how much we appreciate having you as a neighbor. You make us feel welcomed and are always there to help. I couldn't imagine having a better neighbor than you." They clinked bottles before taking their first sips.

"That means a lot John. Thank you," Bud said with a smile.

John went on, "And I've noticed something else about you Bud, a rare quality."

"You're not trying to get me drunk to take advantage of me, are you John?" Bud said as only he could.

Nearly spitting out his beer John assured him, "Don't worry, Abigail is all I can handle. But seriously, what I notice Bud is this, you seem happiest when your friends are happy. In fact, I think sometimes you're happier for them than they are."

With a bit of humility that John had not seen before in Bud, Bud said, "I learned a long time ago 'tis better to give than receive' and 'do unto others as you would have them do unto you.'"

"So you grew up in church?" John inquired with a hint of surprise in his voice.

"Nope, but that doesn't mean I'm not religious. I've seen both statements are true because I put them to the test every day. Over my career I've gotten lots of nice stuff that I appreciate and enjoy. However, nothing made me happier than giving or doing for others and seeing the smiles on their faces. Then I started to realize, there's an unlimited number of people I can do that with. They get joy in the process and so do I. Basically, I can be as happy as I want to be. How cool is that!" Bud exclaimed with his characteristic smile.

John thought for a moment then said, "I grew up going to church but the way you just said that made it more alive, more real, than any pastor I've ever heard."

Taken back a little, Bud said, "Wow, I've never been compared to a pastor before. I think I like beer and Scotch too much to be considered a man of the cloth."

"I think your enjoyment of both is a reflection of your joy for life," John said to affirm Bud.

"Well then, I've really enjoyed life John. Perhaps a little too much sometimes," Bud added with a laugh.

"I think you know this Bud but I'm going to say it anyway because sometimes we need to know we're doing well. You have a good heart and anyone who pays attention can see that," John told him as he looked Bud in the eye.

With a smile, and what John thought might be a tear, not just sweat, Bud replied, "John, that means a tremendous amount to me. Doing good is a reward in and of itself but we're social beings so having connection and affirmation is icing on the cake. Thank you."

That night over dinner John told Abigail about his conversation with Bud. He said, *"At first I looked at reciprocity as a way to get something by doing something for someone first. Then I began to see it as just the right thing to do. Now I see how giving always gets something for you in return if you do it with the right heart. I see with Bud that the gift is joy."*

Abigail smiled as she listened to John as they started clearing the dishes. She could see the wheels in motion as John thought deeply about Bud and what he'd learned.

The Big Surprise!

As they were nearing their second anniversary John came home from a long trip. He'd left for New Mexico Sunday afternoon and it was Friday evening when he walked into the house and set his travel bag down. He was tired but still had the wherewithal to notice something was different. Abigail had candles out, soft music playing, hors d'oeuvres, and a glass of red wine for John. He appreciated the romantic atmosphere, thanked Abigail, and encouraged her to grab a glass and join him. She politely declined and told John she just wanted him to relax after a long trip, which he appreciated.

"So, what went on while I was gone?" He asked. "Save any lives or birth any babies?" he said with a chuckle.

"No lives saved, no babies born," she replied, barely able to keep the smile off her face. "But…" she trailed off.

"Oh no, not but. What's wrong?" John thought to himself, knowing what comes before the word but seldom matters, it's what comes after

that gets all the attention. Did he miss something when he came into the house? Did Abigail get her hair done? Had she lost weight? Was she wearing a new outfit? He was sure he'd missed something that should have been obvious and the hammer was about to fall. "But what?" he sheepishly asked.

"You're going to be a dad," Abigail said with excitement.

John didn't comprehend it at first and innocently asked, "What about my dad?"

"No silly," Abigail replied. She emphasized, "I said *you're* going to be a dad!"

The full weight of the words hit John...he was going to be a father. He was frozen for a moment, but it seemed like an eternity to Abigail. Then he shouted, "I'm going to be a father! You're going to be a mother! We're going to be parents!"

Abigail cried tears of joy and they hugged for several minutes.

They decided to call both sets of parents at the same time to avoid any hint of favoritism. Of course, everyone was excited. They asked about names John and Abigail were considering if they had a boy or girl. They had not thought about names because they'd not slowed down to consider anything other than sharing the good news with family and friends.

After getting off the phone with their parents they walked over to Bud's place. They were eager to share the news and see his excitement knowing how much joy he derived from seeing his friends happy.

"Bud," Abigail started, "John has some important news to tell you."

John wasn't expecting Abigail to pass him the buck so quickly. He stumbled a little when he began, "Yeah Bud, we have some pretty important news to share."

Bud was starting to wonder if John got a promotion and perhaps they were moving so he blurted out, "You're not moving, are you?"

John assured him, "No, nothing like that Bud. We're pretty sure we'll be here for quite a while. You're getting a new neighbor."

"Who's moving?" Bud asked. He couldn't believe someone would be moving and he wouldn't be the first to know.

Abigail chimed in, "No one is moving Bud." John and Abigail were starting to enjoy the moment as they strung Bud along.

"Well, there's no room to build another house," Bud declared.

"No one is moving and no homes are being built Bud, but you will have a new neighbor in about nine months," Abigail told him with the biggest smile you can imagine.

Suddenly it hit Bud, "Holy cow, you're pregnant!"

"Yes, and you're the first person we told after our parents," John said. He went on, "You've been such a good friend and neighbor, and you bring everyone so much joy that we wanted to give you a little joy in return."

Smiling, Bud wiped tears away from his eyes and hugged them both. Then he and John celebrated with some Macallan 18, a nice single malt Scotch that Bud saved for special occasions. Of course, Abigail had to watch John and Bud celebrate but it didn't bother her. All she could think about was the little person inside of her.

The next call that evening was to Duane and Sally. John and Abigail saw them as surrogate parents, soon to be surrogate grandparents. Although it was getting late, John made the call because he didn't want Duane to miss out on the excitement of the moment. He started, "Duane, sorry for calling late but I'll need you to come out of retirement. I have someone who will need your coaching."

"John, I'm flattered but I've hung up my spurs. Other than you, no coaching for me," Duane told him.

"Well, coaching this person will be like coaching me Duane," stringing him along as they'd done with Bud.

"Oh really John. And who else could be like you?" Duane asked with a chuckle.

"Our child," John finally said, revealing the good news.

"Your what?" Duane said. The moment the words were out of his mouth he realized what John was telling him and quickly said, "Oh my. Congratulations to you and Abigail!" Then Duane shouted to Sally who was in the family room, "John and Abigail are pregnant!" Turning back to the phone, Duane told John, "I don't think it's your son or daughter who will need coaching."

They chatted for about 15 minutes and John concluded the call saying, "Duane, any advice you have in this area, I'm all ears."

There were a few more calls to family and close friends. It was late when John and Abigail finally went to bed and they were thankful the next day was Saturday because they were emotionally drained. It had been one of the happiest days of their lives.

The Newest Family Member

It was early June when John and Abigail welcomed Baily into the world. They were both in awe of how tiny she was and how utterly dependent she was on them for everything. It's easy to forget both when you're not around babies.

Determined to be the best parent he could be, John started pondering how he might put into practice much of the psychology he was learning on his life journey. He'd taken some time off work to help Abigail and spend time getting to know his little girl. During breakfast he shared with Abigail what he was thinking so they would both be on the same page.

After taking a bite of bacon he started the conversation, "Abigail, have you ever heard of *choice architecture*?"

"That's not a term I'm familiar with," she replied while nursing Baily.

"It's something I've been reading about lately. I'm finding it extremely helpful with customers and I think it will be good to use with Baily. Imagine she's four years old and you innocently ask, 'What do you want to do today?' That can be risky because she might suggest something you can't do or don't feel up to doing that day," he shared.

"You mean like horseback riding or flying in an airplane?" she said with a laugh as she stared into Baily's eyes as she nursed.

"Exactly," John said. After a sip of orange juice, he went on, "No matter what you suggest after that, everything is compared to horses and airplanes so she'll be upset at not getting her way."

"I remember those days as a little girl. How can we avoid that trap?" Abigail inquired. By now Baily's belly was full and Abigail was rocking her to sleep.

"Instead of the open-ended question, give her a few acceptable choices. Ask, 'Honey, would you like to go to the movies, to the library for reading time, or to the playground after lunch?' This approach gives her choices, a sense of freedom and ownership. Whatever she chooses to do, she'll be happier than if she felt forced."

"That's so simple but brilliant John," Abigail said with a smile. Then she asked him, "How can I use that approach at work? It would be helpful and allow me to practice."

"What do you have trouble getting people to do at the office?" John asked as he got up to put his dishes in the dishwasher.

"Two big challenges are getting people to take their meds and do their exercises," she quickly shared as she continued to rock Baily.

"Hmmm. With meds does it matter what time of day they're taken?" he asked as he watched her holding Baily.

"Most of the time it doesn't matter, it's just getting them to take them with some consistency each day," Abigail told him.

"Well, try this, 'Mr. Jones, do you think you'll take your medicine with breakfast, lunch, or dinner?' That's giving him *options and ownership.* Let's say he tells you he'll take them every day at lunch. You can reinforce his commitment with, 'Mr. Jones I'm going to hold you to that lunchtime choice and ask you about it next time you're in, okay?' When he tells you that's fine, he's even more committed to the choice he freely made. If he's like most people, he doesn't want to be the kind of person who says one thing but does another. And he doesn't want to look bad in your eyes when he's in the office for his follow-up visit. Make sense?" he concluded.

"Totally!" Abigail exclaimed. "That last part about not feeling bad, I've heard you talk about that before. What's the term you use?"

"In psychology it's called the principle of consistency. People feel an internal psychological pressure and external social pressure to be consistent in what they say and do. It's not hard to engage it. Rather than

telling people what to do, ask questions instead. For example, don't say, 'Get me that patient report before lunch.' Go with, 'Can you get me that patient report by lunch?'"

"*What if they say no?*" she asked in a concerned tone.

"*That's a possibility so I always try to give myself fallback positions.* Instead of asking for the report by noon, ask for it by 9:00 a.m. If the person says they can't get it by 9:00 a.m. then ask if there's any way they can get it to you by 10:00 a.m. People hate to say no repeatedly so I've learned that anticipating no and having fallback positions ready in the moment usually gets me what I need within an acceptable time frame. *This is another way to engage reciprocity because when you concede a little people usually concede a little in return,*" John shared.

Getting up to put Baily in her bassinet Abigail mentioned another advantage, "*When you ask and are willing to negotiate a little you seem a lot more reasonable than the person who just makes demands of others.* I bet that's a big reason people respond to you as well as they do."

"You know, I never considered that, but I think you're right. See, I'm not the one doing all the teaching," he told her with a smile as she walked out of the room.

They'd started off talking about raising Baily but also came up with lots of new ways for Abigail to tap into the concepts at work. Influence was helping John succeed and she knew those same approaches could help her too.

New States

Things were progressing quite nicely in the Southwest Region for MediTech. Sales were up with current clients and John had brought on new clients in each of the three states. It was a combination of Duane's training and John's approach to people. Cathy Metcalf was still the VP of Sales & Marketing and John's boss. She called him one day to discuss a big change coming down the pike.

"Hi John, it's Cathy. Got a minute?" she asked as soon as she heard his voice.

"I'll give you two minutes Cathy, 100% more time than you asked for," he joked.

"Sold!" she said. "John, we have a big initiative coming and it's going to impact you. Are you up for a challenge?"

Normally a little reserved, he threw caution to the wind because Cathy and the company had been so good to him. "I'm always up for a challenge Cathy. How can I help?"

"Things are going so well in the region and our brand recognition is growing so we'd like to expand into Utah and Nevada," she told him. "We realize this will require a lot from you and we know that won't be easy with a new child at home. We assure you the plan is not for you to handle five states by yourself. What we'd like you to do is devote one week a month to those new states to begin opening them up. By this time next year we should have another half dozen trainees and we'd like to send one to work with you just like you did with Duane."

"So, this is a two-year commitment; one to open the states and another to coach the future rep?" he asked.

"Yes, the plan is the new person would eventually move to Salt Lake City or Las Vegas and take responsibility for both states," Cathy told John.

"Cathy, let me give it some thought. May I get back to you tomorrow?" he asked.

Cathy replied, "Fair enough."

The next day he called Cathy, "My biggest concern is the time commitment required to maintain the current region and open up two states. If this means taking one of my weeks on the road and devoting that week to the new states, I think I can handle it. Is that how you envision it, less time in Arizona and New Mexico so I have the time for Utah and Nevada?"

"Yes John, that's how we see it working. We're not asking you to work an extra week in overtime. We're asking you because we know your relationships with clients in those states are strong enough that we'll maintain our position. We think the region will ultimately take a big leap forward after Nevada and Utah are up and running, then another leap with a dedicated rep."

"Is there anything else the change will entail?" he asked.

"We're toying with the idea of having the rep report to you once he or she is settled in and working independently. It will give you management experience. Long term, and this is well down the road, if this works we might take the same approach with California, Oregon, and Washington."

"Wow, that's ambitious," John said.

"Well, you've opened our eyes to what's possible if we hire the right people and have the right coaching in place," she responded.

"One last question," John started. "It didn't escape my notice that you never said 'I' but always said 'we'. Who else is part of 'we'?"

"Bob McMillen," she said. Bob was the new CEO who'd taken the helm at MediTech earlier that year. He came from a competitor and had a reputation for taking companies to the next level. In MediTech's case that meant ultimately having representation in all 50 states and becoming a publicly traded company. John met Bob a couple of times when he was back for sales meetings. Although he didn't feel like he knew Bob, Cathy assured John that Bob knew him. She went on, "John, this is really Bob's brainchild. He's more aggressive than I would have been and he's the boss. Not only is this important for us, but it's also a huge opportunity for you."

This changed the situation a little so John asked if Cathy would be okay arranging a meeting for the three of them. John wanted to get to know Bob a little better and lay out how he thought they should go about this.

Cathy was always one to promote her people and she appreciated John's moxie. She asked if he would be willing to fly to Charlotte to spend time with her and Bob. She knew the more Bob got to know John the more confident he would be about John's approach. John agreed and they found time in the coming weeks for a two-day trip.

Back to the Home Office

An Uncomfortable Conversation

It was a few weeks after his call with Cathy that John was in the bedroom packing his bags for the trip to Charlotte. Abigail waltzed into the room feeling upbeat. She had just put Baily down for a late morning nap. She went right to sleep so Abigail was doing her own little victory dance. She noticed John was packing his nicest suits and innocently asked, "Going to see some new clients this week?"

"No, why do you ask?" John said as he put his dress shoes and socks in the travel bag.

"You're packing your best suits," Abigail mentioned, showing her attention to detail.

"I'm going to Charlotte to meet with Cathy and Bob McMillen, the new CEO," he said in a distracted tone.

"Wow, sounds important. What's the big occasion?" She inquired.

"It's about the new state expansion and training a new rep," he told her as he picked out his shirts and ties.

"What state expansion?" she replied with concern in her voice.

At that moment John realized he'd not mentioned any of this to her and the look on his face betrayed that truth. He turned to her and said, "I thought I told you about this. They want me to expand the region into Nevada and Utah. In about a year I'll train a new rep to take over those states just like Duane trained me."

"Sounds like a pretty big decision on your part. It also seems like it might be a big-time commitment. Why didn't you discuss any of it with me?" she asked.

John could sense the disappointment in her voice. Suddenly he was disappointed in himself. "I'm sorry," he said. "The way it was explained to me, it won't be any more time away from home. Any time on the road will just be shifted to the new states for a while. I felt like it was simply a new task, something that wouldn't impact us at all. Believe me, if I thought it would mean more time away from home, or additional stress, especially with having a child now, I would not have agreed to it."

"I believe you John. What disappoints me is that you didn't think to run any of this by me. That's what partners do," she said as she averted her gaze. Her feelings were hurt, and John knew it. He reiterated how sorry he was and promised to do better in the future. Neither felt good as he left for the airport. They had so few disagreements that whenever they popped up it left both feeling uneasy. Intense emotions take time to wane so it was probably good that each had some time alone to process everything.

Free Isn't Necessarily a Gift

On his way to the MediTech headquarters to meet with Bob and Cathy, John went out of his way at the airport to track down Colleen, his gate agent friend. He knew seeing her would help him feel a little better. Traveling can be lonely, so it was always nice to see a friendly face, especially because Colleen was so upbeat. He made himself inconspicuous in line so he could surprise her. When he stepped up to the counter she was looking down so he said, "Can I rebook these tickets for Hawaii?" knowing that would grab her attention and make her laugh. He always made it a point to say hello if she was working. It also gave him a chance to give her an update on his father. He would never forget her help on that first solo business trip and her kindness when his father suffered a stroke. It meant a lot to Colleen that John always kept her up on his dad's health. Those bonding experiences coupled with John's frequent travel helped them form a friendship.

It was late Sunday afternoon when John arrived in Charlotte and made his way to the Doubletree Hotel. With all his visits to the headquarters over the years the Doubletree felt familiar, almost like a home away from home. As is the case with most Doubletree guests, John looked forward to the warm chocolate chip cookie the clerk would hand him when he checked in. He'd stayed at a lot of hotels during his travels, but he felt different about the Doubletree. He wondered why and then it hit him.

Most hotels were nice and had freebies for guests. For example, other hotels had cookies and often a variety to choose from. Those cookies were typically set near the front door so hotel guests could grab as many as they wanted whenever they entered or left the hotel.

It was the hotel's act of giving that created his feelings. Anything free was nice but not everything that was free felt like a gift. Reciprocity was engaged the moment guests accepted the chocolate chip cookie from the hotel staff at check in. It set the tone for the rest of the stay.

Being given a cookie was a little act of kindness that produced outsized results. Hotels were usually clustered in areas John traveled to and he would go out of his way to stay at Doubletrees if the price and distance made sense for MediTech and his clients.

He started pondering how he might use the Doubletree approach to quickly form relationships with potential new clients in Nevada and Utah as they opened the states up. He knew just telling people about the MediTech website wouldn't cut it. That would be analogous to cookies at the door, help yourself whenever you want. There was certainly a place for that self-serve aspect because clients want to access information when they need it rather than depending on whether they could reach a real live person. He also knew trinkets like MediTech pens wouldn't do either. There had to be a way for John to engage reciprocity in a meaningful way with clients as the Doubletree did with their cookies. It was something he decided to give more thought to because it could help with the new state roll out.

Influencing the CEO

John felt different as he walked into the MediTech headquarters on this trip. The first time he visited he was interviewing for a job. Everything was new and overwhelming that day. Next he was there as a trainee, focused on soaking up as much information as he could. Even after becoming a sales rep he was still the new kid on the block. Now, with more than five years under his belt, he was there to get a new assignment and share his advice on how to expand the Southwest Region for MediTech with his boss and the CEO.

There are times in life when you feel grown up and for John some of those times included heading off to college, starting his first job, moving to Dallas, marrying Abigail, then buying a house. Most recently it was becoming a father. Now his company was seeking his advice and he felt like a respected peer.

John's old golf coach used to tell the team, *"Luck is where preparation meets opportunity."* Later John learned it was Seneca, the Roman philosopher who first uttered those words, but he still told everyone it was his golf coach because of the influence "Coach" had on him. He took those words to heart and was ready for this opportunity with Bob and Cathy. He spent time talking with people about the opportunities he saw in the new territory and to seek their advice. He grilled Duane on what he might do differently if he had a redo on opening the Southwest Region. He made calls to his original mentors – Ben, Francesca, Russell, and Nancy – with specific questions he knew they could answer based on their strengths. Finally, he leaned on a few clients, especially Al and Dr. Michaels, for insights on what MediTech could do to engage prospective clients in new states. As he reflected on his preparation he realized again his misstep with Abigail. He wished he'd talked with her about this big opportunity. He usually leaned on her wisdom and the fact that she worked on the frontline of the healthcare industry would have been most helpful.

The meeting was conducted in Bob's office. It was on the top floor of the headquarters with windows on three sides that afforded spectacular views of the North, East, and West. The office was spacious and elaborately furnished, almost like a penthouse apartment. On the walls were pictures of Bob with celebrities, various government officials, and the current governor of the state. It was all a bit over the top for John based on his middle class, Midwestern upbringing but he quickly oriented himself so they could get down to business.

John knew it was always good to start meetings with customers by letting them do most of the talking while he listened attentively. He focused his listening skills by remembering a simple acronym: **STARS**. It reminded him to *Stop everything he was doing so he could give full attention, focus on Tone of voice because it usually indicated mood, Ask clarifying questions, Restate in his own words what he thought he heard, and Scribble notes so he wouldn't miss important points.*

This approach worked well with Bob because he was a driver personality who liked to feel in control of the situations he was in. All of John's customer interactions taught him that good questions followed by attentive listening were analogous to the rudder of a ship, they steer the conversation while allowing the other person to feel in control of the dialogue. *John was savvy enough to know the principle of consistency was at play in that, the more Bob felt any idea they agreed on was Bob's, the more Bob would back John's plan for Nevada and Utah.*

Another approach John employed was to shoot for the sun, moon, and stars. Too many people censor themselves because they're afraid of rejection. John asked for everything he wanted because, as Duane had reminded him, the worst that could happen was to hear no but then he would be ready with several acceptable fallback positions to retreat to. *This was an application of reciprocity – concede a little in the moment to come across as reasonable and quite often people will concede a little in response.*

Before the meeting ended John was smiling wide inside as he realized he was going to get nearly everything he'd hoped for and a few extras that he didn't expect. The extras were Bob's ideas and amounted to icing on the cake. When the meeting ended Cathy and John made their way to the elevator. As the elevator doors closed Cathy asked if John would join her in her office, which he was happy to do. When they arrived she closed the door and invited him to have a seat. Settling into her leather chair behind the cherry wood desk she started the conversation, "John, you're unbelievable! I've never seen anybody work Bob the way you did."

John always felt comfortable with Cathy and casually replied, "Cathy, I can understand why you might say that but let me assure you, I didn't work Bob. If someone heard that they might think I manipulated him for my own gain. You gave me an opportunity and I took a thoughtful approach to positively influence the situation."

With an inquisitive look Cathy said, "I'm curious. Tell me about your approach."

John began to share, *"First, I spent time thinking about the opportunity. Next, I wrote down a few ideas. After that, I shared my ideas with people I respect because I wanted their advice. Finally, I put together a plan to ethically influence Bob in the direction I believed would be best for the company and future clients.* Don't you think what we agreed to will be best for MediTech, the new rep we'll hire soon, and clients we'll take on in both states?"

"There's no doubt everyone will win if we can pull it off," she told John.

Thinking about what he learned when negotiating for the house, John told Cathy, "A wise person taught me not long ago, whenever I propose something I should aim for this: *Good for you, good for me, then we're good to go. It's the best way to create win-win deals.*"

Cathy followed up by saying, "John, I'm going to give you something else to think about. Once we get Nevada and Utah up and running I'd like you to consider coming into the headquarters occasionally to do a little training. People at every level and in all positions in the company could benefit from your wisdom. In addition, it would be great for your career to get that kind of exposure here in the headquarters."

John clearly saw this would be an opportunity to pay it forward and fulfill his promise to Duane. "I'm flattered and would enjoy that Cathy...once we get this expansion behind us," he said with a smile.

John had dinner with a few coworkers then made his way back to the hotel. He called Abigail before bed to share the good news about the meeting with Bob and Cathy. As always, she was happy for him, but he could detect a hint of concern in her voice. He assumed it was a hangover from their conversation a few days earlier so he didn't mention the future opportunity Cathy talked about because he thought it might be too much on the heels of that discussion. He asked Abigail if everything was okay. She assured him it was nothing and that they could talk when he got home.

The Doctor Visit

It was late Thursday night when John walked in the door with his travel bag and suitcase in hand. He was mentally and physically exhausted from the combination of travel, the big meeting, and the way he'd left the house a few days before.

Abigail was exhausted too but for a different reason. She was still up, sitting on the couch in the family room waiting for John to get home so she could talk with him. Before John could say anything Abigail said, "John, what happened earlier this week is resolved in my mind. That's not why I waited up for you. I didn't mention anything about what I'm going to share when we spoke yesterday evening because I didn't want to dampen your excitement. I'm happy for you."

Suddenly John was concerned and it showed on his face as he sat down next to her on the couch. Abigail took a deep breath then continued, "Something happened yesterday and I'm scared. I was doing some chores after I put Baily down for her morning nap when out of nowhere I felt a sharp pain in the back of my head. It was like an explosion and I dropped to my knees. I've never felt anything that intense before and I'm concerned because my cousin Karla had brain surgery years ago. I think it was due to an aneurysm."

In the space of a moment their conversation from days before, his meeting in Charlotte, and future career opportunities meant nothing. Being in the medical field John and Abigail knew this was not something to take lightly. Fortunately, because of their connections they were able to see a doctor the next morning at 10:00 a.m.

They held hands as they entered the doctor's office and gave their name to the nurse behind the desk. Soon enough they were in a sterile waiting room anxiously anticipating the doctor's arrival. Eventually the doctor came in, quickly introduced herself, glanced at the medical chart in her hand, then turned to Abigail to get more details. Abigail quickly shared what happened and her fear because of her cousin's brain surgery. Naturally the doctor was concerned when she heard about the aneurysm. She started to suggest a series of tests but before she could finish she was paged and had to leave the room for a few minutes.

When the doctor stepped away John and Abigail talked more about the situation. John asked if Abigail was certain her cousin suffered an aneurysm. She said it was quite a few years ago, before she entered the medical field, so she wasn't 100% sure. They both knew it would be important to know exactly what happened because family history could affect the doctor's diagnosis and potential treatment options.

Abigail called Karla right away and explained what happened a few days before. She told Karla they were at the hospital and needed to know the circumstances around Karla's surgery. Much to Abigail's relief, Karla said it wasn't an aneurysm. She'd fallen off a horse, hit her head and experienced brain swelling as a result. To reduce the pressure she had emergency surgery. Fortunately, there were no long-term ramifications from the fall or the surgery.

They were both somewhat relieved at Karla's news. The doctor returned and apologized for having to step away, explaining she had a patient who was in recovery from a recent procedure and the nurse on call had a question about the patient's meds.

Abigail told the doctor about the phone conversation and that her cousin did not have an aneurysm. As she listened, arms folded while leaning against the wall, the doctor shook her head slightly. She said, "I hear what you're saying but I can't get an aneurysm out of my mind. I still suggest we do the tests just to be safe."

John interjected, "So just to be clear; if we had not accidentally mentioned the aneurysm and correctly told you about the fall, you would not suggest the tests?"

"That's right," the doctor replied. "I know it's not completely rational, but I couldn't live with myself if I let you leave without those tests and something happened to Abigail."

John saw the concern on Abigail's face and knew instinctively this wasn't the time or place to question the doctor any further. Almost immediately, looking at Abigail and not the doctor, he replied, "Let's run the tests just to be safe."

When the doctor stepped out again Abigail sighed a sense of relief and thanked John for not pursuing the matter further. The doubt, no matter how small, would plague her so she was glad they decided to proceed with the recommended tests. As they hoped, and the doctor expected, the tests came back clear. It was determined Abigail must have experienced a severe migraine.

John thought about that interaction with the doctor for a long time. *He was familiar with biases and how they can lead us astray into seemingly irrational behaviors. As much as anyone, doctors are logical people who rely on science, not feelings or intuition, when treating patients, but even doctors are not immune to their own occasionally flawed thinking.* It made John wonder how many decisions he made on a typical day that seemed rational but were driven by forces beyond his conscious thinking. He decided to do a little research on the topic.

Everyone has Biases

Much to everyone's relief the doctor was correct; Abigail simply had an intense migraine. There were no lingering effects and they quickly returned to life as usual but John couldn't forget the interaction with the doctor. It had a profound impact on him so in his spare time he began to pursue his study of biases.

He learned biases were mental shortcuts all people used to one degree or another. They operate below the surface of conscious thought and happen so quickly that people are not aware of how they impact their decisions. Quite often these biases lead people to make seemingly irrational choices but in predictable ways. Because of the predictability John knew, learning everything he could about biases would help him understand people even better.

He quickly recognized these shortcuts served humans well for the most part over the course of evolution because they saved time and energy. In the not too distant past, life and death might have been on the line, so time and energy were precious commodities. However, the modern world presents challenges where biases don't always help; and, on some occasions biases can work against you.

Take confirmation bias for instance. This bias kicks in when individuals look for information to confirm what they already believe. It takes a lot less effort to do this than exploring all the reasons you might be wrong. Throw on top of that the reality that nobody likes to admit they're wrong and you can see how confirmation bias becomes a powerful hidden force. But, with so much information coming at people every day this shortcut often results in less than optimal decisions.

Another bias is the preference for "in group" people. It's natural for humans to gravitate towards people who look like them, sound like them, and have other qualities that are similar. Over evolution these similarities likely indicated a friend, not foe. A quick, accurate decision to determine who was a friend and who was an enemy could have been the difference between life and death in the past. However, that wasn't usually the case in the 21st century so this bias often led to unwarranted discrimination of out group people.

John started to make the connection back to the influence principles he first learned about in college. Each was a mental shortcut, a heuristic, to yes that helped humans survive and thrive over the course of history.

For example, *it's easier to say yes to people you consider friends (liking) or that you feel a special bond with (unity) versus a stranger even though safety isn't necessarily on the line in this day and age.*

He also knew it was natural to say yes to people who first helped him (reciprocity). A willingness to help someone who helped him was a no brainer – literally. This principle also helped humans survive and thrive because people could accomplish more by working together. Of course, this opens people up to returning the favor even when the "help" or "gift" they first received wasn't necessarily wanted.

People didn't need to be taught there's safety in numbers and that following the crowd (social proof) usually resulted in positive outcomes. Now that information spreads so quickly, social proof can be reached faster than ever, sometimes to our detriment if the information that's so readily accepted is incomplete or even false.

Nor did individuals need to be taught to follow the lead of an expert (authority). Once people learn someone is an authority, they automatically give more weight to their advice than someone who isn't viewed as an expert. With so many self-proclaimed gurus these days it's easy for people to be bamboozled.

Keeping your word had a built-in reinforcement mechanism – a good feeling – that drove the need to be consistent (consistency) more than just looking good to others. Even if someone didn't acknowledge keeping your word, you could still feel good about yourself knowing your words and deeds were in alignment. The problem is, people sometimes make small commitments that lead them to bigger commitments they didn't anticipate. Commitments that can be hard to adjust.

And John realized nobody had to teach him fear of loss (scarcity) was a much bigger driver to yes than a potential gain. That decision process came as naturally as the others. Politicians and news outlets play on this principle quite a bit, often stoking fear needlessly to win votes or gain viewers.

While these quick, systematic decision processes were helpful over the course of evolution and usually are most of the time now, they can get people in trouble when manipulative individuals understand how to use the biases to take advantage of others.

For John, trying to understand all this psychology highlighted the nagging thought that it was like putting a puzzle together. He'd mentioned that idea years ago when he first met Duane. He remembered Duane commenting that John's view was more of a philosophy to live by than some sales technique. Techniques are like the parts of an engine, each has a purpose, but when all the parts work together you have a machine which is far more powerful than any of its individual parts. Just as you hope the operator of a powerful piece of machinery is careful, he was seeing more clearly how important it was to ethically wield his understanding of human psychology because of its immense power to direct the thoughts and behavior of people.

Sage Advice

Avoid Stinking Thinking

John stayed in regular touch with Duane. Besides their close friendship, John leaned on Duane as a mentor, someone he could use as a sounding board for ideas. Because Duane knew the business so intimately his insights were always valuable. As the time drew close for John to implement his plans for Utah and Nevada he got together with Duane for coffee.

The cafe where they met was a regular stop before they used to head out for sales calls. It had been many years since John's first time there. Everyone working knew him and Duane and they, in turn, knew all the baristas by name.

After grabbing their caffeine fixes and some danishes they settled into familiar seats near the window so they could enjoy a little people watching as they talked. John confessed that despite his successes, and what Duane might observe on the outside, he was nervous about opening the new states.

John's admission prompted Duane to ask, "Can you describe what you mean by nervous?"

"Come on Duane, you know what being nervous is," John replied, acting as if Duane was pulling his leg.

Duane stared at John and patiently said, "John, I want to know what your thoughts and feelings are that you've labeled nerves."

John started to describe what he was thinking and feeling about Nevada and Utah. He went on longer than he expected and when he'd exhausted himself, Duane interjected, "All that you just described I felt when I opened up Texas for the company I was with prior to Medi-Tech. However, everything changed with Arizona and New Mexico. That's because a wise friend gave me some good counsel and I'm going to share that wisdom with you. Keri told me those same thoughts and feelings could be reframed as excitement. The more I pondered it the more I realized she was right. When I began to reframe my nerves to excitement I started looking forward to all the tasks associated with opening those two states. *How you label things in your mind makes a big difference.* Do you hear what I'm saying John?"

"I've never considered that before. I don't think I'm much different from other people in that I don't look forward to activities I'm nervous about. But I do look forward to things I'm excited about," John replied. The wheels in his mind were spinning as he looked out the window.

"Exactly!" Duane exclaimed as he sipped his coffee. "Every time those sensations come up, I encourage you to tell yourself, 'I'm so excited!' It will feel weird and unnatural at first, just like you told me it was unnatural trying to implement changes to your golf swing after taking lessons with a pro. In this case it might even feel like you're lying to yourself but you're not. You're simply reframing something you never consciously learned. You can do that with all your other thoughts and feelings. *In that sense we're the architects of our own lives.*"

Putting down his croissant John told Duane, "That reminds me of a quote I read once from Abraham Lincoln. He said, 'Most folks are about as happy as they make up their minds to be.'"

"Honest Abe wouldn't lie John," Duane said with a chuckle. Finishing his coffee, he went on, "I try to avoid 'stinking thinking.' Consider all that comes in through our senses. We get to interpret the meaning. For example, are sunny days good or bad?"

John answered, "I guess it depends. If you want to golf you think sunny days are great. However, if it's not rained for weeks and your grass is turning brown then perhaps a sunny day isn't what you were hoping for."

"That's right. Shakespeare put it best when he said, *'There's nothing either good or bad but thinking makes it so.'* Consider this: when someone passes away grief is natural. However, some people cannot get beyond grief while others choose to focus on how happy they were to have known the person. Sure, they'll miss the person they lost but their focus is happiness, not sadness. Each of us can make that choice moment by moment, day by day. It seems hard at first because you must break old mental habits but it's so worth it. Disciplining your mind that way benefits you and everyone you come in contact with."

It was then, sitting in the coffee shop, that John resolved to do his best to take every thought captive. Later that evening, after putting Baily to bed, he shared what Duane taught him with Abigail. He asked her to hold him accountable to look on the bright side. *He added a daily ritual, a positive affirmation, to his morning routine.* Shortly after waking up, he would say out loud, *"Today will be a good day because I will approach everything with a positive attitude and I will learn from every situation."*

He realized, even if he wasn't looking at something in a positive light, he could catch himself and ask, "What can I learn from this?" With this approach he was still being true to himself and his goal of right thinking. Suddenly he was feeling excited about tackling Nevada and Utah and he had Duane to thank for it.

Be Memorable

"It's all showbiz. We're not selling steaks, we're selling the sizzle," This memorable insight came from Clyde, a sales executive, who taught John's training class during his MediTech orientation. John used this memorable insight as he got ready to start making prospecting calls in the new states.

As John pondered that saying he recalled Clyde was full of unforgettable quips that drove home truisms about selling. An organized pack rat, John fished through his old MediTech training materials and found his notes from Clyde's presentations. He chuckled as he read his notes and envisioned Clyde telling his stories. Among John's favorites were:

- *"If it's raining soup, hold up your bowl."* It's a silly but memorable word picture telling us to take advantage of opportunities when they present themselves.
- *"Self-interest isn't the only horse in the race, but it is the one to bet on."* Most people are concerned about themselves. That's not good or bad, it's just the way we're built, so take it into consideration whenever you're trying to persuade someone.
- *"Don't sell past the close."* You may have ten points to cover but if you hear "Yes" after three or four...shut up or else you might talk yourself out of a sale.
- *"I may be the best player on the team, but I can't play every position."* When you're leading, you need to rely on your team. Do everything you can to make them better players and you'll all be better off.
- *"When all you have to sell are bananas, sell bananas."* Rather than focusing on what you don't have, learn to leverage whatever you do have.

Other valuable sayings that stuck with John from his time in the industry included:

- *"Good for you, good for me, then we're good to go."* This one he learned from Joe when they bought their home. Always make sure you're doing right by people.
- *"There's nothing high or low but comparing makes it so."* He picked up this one when he read Brian Ahearn's book *Influence PEOPLE*. Customers will always say your price is too high, but the question is, "Compared to what?"

- *"When you say it, they doubt it. When they say it, they believe it."* John came across this Tom Hopkins quote in his book *How to Master the Art of Selling*. Telling someone what to do will never gain as much buy-in as it will if they come up with the idea themselves. This means asking the right questions.
- *"You can have everything you want in life if you will just help enough other people get what they want."* This Zig Ziglar quote goes to the heart of reciprocity. Help people succeed and you'll build an army of people who want to help you succeed in return.
- *"The more I practice the luckier I get."* As a golfer John recalled Arnold Palmer saying this. It tied in with his old coach's advice, *"Luck is where preparation meets opportunity."*
- *"Don't give to get but if you don't give, you'll never get."* This was John's quote. It sums up the motivation for reciprocity while recognizing the reality that you shouldn't expect people to give unless you give first.
- *"Less is more."* Don't overwhelm people with choices. Psychologist Barry Schwartz pointed out that choice is good, but too many choices confuse the brain and make it harder for people to decide.

Working the Plan

For a month John had systematically been reaching out to medical practices in Nevada and Utah. He hired an old college friend to make it happen. Rick was an IT guru who started his own company, Doctor Hospital Data, a few years earlier. The company mined data related to health care providers and put it into usable formats. Rick's work saved John countless hours because, rather than having to dig up information himself, with one click of the mouse Rick was able to provide John with the name of every medical practice in both states along with every physician who worked in each practice.

Names, emails, and mailing addresses were all that John needed to get rolling.

John's plan was simple: start creating brand awareness in Nevada and Utah for MediTech and himself. The goal was to pre-suade doctors, getting them receptive to John and MediTech, so they'd be excited to meet him when he started traveling to each state. He recalled from his Psych 101 class that *people are more likely to say yes to people they're familiar with. According to one study, familiarity could be as simple as seeing someone's photograph repeatedly so he made sure to include his picture on every communication he sent.* He took this idea one step further by creating a series of short videos. Knowing attention is a precious commodity, and that people can only focus on one piece of information at a time, he kept each video under 60 seconds.

In his initial video he briefly introduced himself and made sure to include Abigail and Baily. He did this because he knew the more people saw him as a regular person with a family, similar to many of them, the more likely they'd be to want to meet him in person.

During week two he highlighted more about his professional background and MediTech. Likability was a door opener but that would only get him so far. At the end of the day people wanted to know what he and MediTech could do to help them. He tapped into his expertise and MediTech's by leaning on client testimonials.

Many of his Texas clients happily joined John in the videos to share a little about their experience working with him and MediTech. *Third party testimonials are an application of the principle of authority and social proof. Using a third party is always better than talking about yourself and your company because prospective customers know you have a vested interest in both. Third parties can make statements about you and/or your company that build you up and sound perfectly natural, not braggadocious.*

Week three teased people with specifics about MediTech products. Again, John might be likable, but physicians needed to know how MediTech products would help them. They always had medical supply reps who wanted their time so why was MediTech different? *Knowing people are more motivated by what they may lose or are missing, John made sure he highlighted what physician's current products might be missing when compared to MediTech products.*

After building excitement, in week four John announced he would be in both states the following week. *While he wanted to meet with everyone, he let them know his time would be limited and that he would only be able to meet with a dozen health providers during that first visit to the new state. That honest application of scarcity grabbed people's attention and before he knew it, he'd received nearly two dozen requests for meetings.*

One other aspect of the plan was *connecting with people on LinkedIn. This was another chance for people to see his face, learn about his background, and to start a conversation.* Not only was John not lazy, but he also knew how to capture attention, so he didn't go with the standard "I'd like to connect with you" default message. Instead, he included some variation of the following personal message to everyone he reached out to.

Name,
If my name is familiar, it's probably because I've sent you a few emails. I'm a rep for MediTech Supplies and we're entering the state so I thought I'd reach out. I'd like to connect with you if you're open to it.

Sincerely,
John

Within days of sending his messages John was making lots of new connections in Nevada and Utah. *Each time someone accepted his request to connect he shot back a short message thanking them for connecting. A good number of people responded to that thank you message and quite often conversations ensued.* John knew every touch point was helping to build his likability, familiarity, and authority.

The Elephant in the Room

What Happens in Vegas

John couldn't believe how quickly that first year in Nevada and Utah went by. Despite a little more time on the road than he anticipated, he enjoyed traveling throughout both states because of the natural beauty each possessed. He liked the people he met and realized he learned valuable lessons opening a new territory from scratch.

Now he was about to tackle another first. He was going to take a new sales rep under his wing. He thought about the impact Duane had on him professionally and personally, and hoped he could be the same resource for the new rep.

It was early fall when John met Paul for the first time. To say Medi-Tech was high on Paul would have been an understatement. He was an Ivy League graduate who'd played football until a knee injury shortened his career midway through the season during his junior year. It was during rehab that Paul became interested in the medical field. He thought about going to medical school to become a physician. He took his MCATs but decided against med school because he was burned out on studying and med school was a bigger time commitment than he was willing to make. Being competitive and ambitious he decided to get into the medical field on the sales side. He spent a few years with a much larger competitor, starting with inside sales. He moved to MediTech because of the opportunity for an outside sales role. The possibility of taking over Nevada and Utah while living in Las Vegas held appeal as well.

Deep down John felt a little intimidated by Paul. Here was a tall, good looking, athletic Ivy League grad who was full of energy and ideas, someone people seemed to naturally gravitate to. John wondered if Duane ever felt intimidated by him in the beginning. The plan was to have Paul live in Dallas for a year so he could shadow John daily as John had done with Duane. Each month John and Paul would hop on a plane and make their way to Nevada or Utah.

On their first trip John tracked down Colleen so Paul could meet her. He told Paul the story about how John and Colleen met and how helpful she was when his father had his stroke. He emphasized Paul needed to treat everyone as important because they are. On top of that, you never know how someone might help you in the future.

John and Paul were different and that was highlighted on their first trip. Paul was younger, single, and wanted to play as soon as the workday was over. John was never much of a partier, not even in college. Now he was in his late 20s, married, a father, and career focused. All of this made his decisions about free time outside of work quite different from Paul's. Nonetheless, he said he'd go out with Paul because it was Paul's first trip to Las Vegas.

John said, "Paul, I have to tell you, partying isn't my style. It never really was and now that I'm married and have a child it's even less appealing. However, I know this is your first visit to Vegas so I'll head out with you, but we have to be back at the hotel by 10:00 p.m. Deal?"

"Deal!" Paul shot back.

They stopped by a couple of well-known spots on the strip and John noticed Paul had two beers for every one he had. True to his word, around 9:45 p.m. John told Paul it was time to make their way back to the hotel. Paul protested at first. "Oh come on John, you sound a little like my parents. We're having harmless fun so let's stay a while longer."

John realized he had a decision to make. He could stick to his word or cave to Paul. He knew his job wasn't to be Paul's drinking buddy. Rather, John needed to do everything he could to get Paul ready to take over a territory where he would be responsible for millions of dollars of sales.

Finishing his beer, John said in a confident tone, "Paul, believe me, I'm not saying we need to leave because I think I'm one of your parents. We're out here to do a job and we have to be sharp in the morning so we need to be rested and ready to go." Disappointed, Paul conceded as he chugged a nearly full beer. John paid the bill and they grabbed a cab back to the hotel.

John was up early as usual and made his way down to the hotel gym. He wasn't running races anymore but he liked to hop on a treadmill or go outside for a run each day to get his blood flowing first thing in the morning. When he was racing he read a lot of books on running and what stuck with him was the impact aerobic activity had on the brain. It was almost a wonder drug so no matter how tired he was, running for at least 30 minutes each morning was a priority. The night before he told Paul about what he'd learned and invited Paul to join him in the morning but Paul was nowhere to be found when John walked into the fitness area at 6:30 a.m.

It was 8:15 a.m., about ten minutes before they were supposed to head out for their first appointment and Paul was still absent. Finally, John called him to find out where he was. He could hear the grogginess in Paul's voice and assumed he had just gotten up. Within 15 minutes Paul was in the lobby but he was late and John could tell he was nursing a hangover.

Again, John was faced with holding to what he felt was right or letting this slip. He knew if he let it slip it was more likely to happen again. His reputation was on the line so he decided it was too important to ignore.

"Paul, did you go back out last night?" he asked in a direct manner.

A little embarrassed, Paul said, "I didn't go out. I hung out at the hotel bar watching ball games."

"How long were you down there?" John asked.

"The MSU - ISU game went into overtime, so it was about 2:00 a.m. when I left," Paul replied as he pretended to look at his watch.

"You closed down the bar? Paul, I'm going to be straight with you. I like you and see tremendous potential with you. Cathy and others at MediTech see it too. You're a smart, good looking, athletic guy with an engaging personality. People naturally gravitate to you and your Ivy League background gives you instant credibility. But behavior like you displayed last night isn't going to cut it. Everything I just praised you for are only door openers. If you don't take this job seriously, know our products inside and out, and learn about our clients you're going to fall flat on your face. That will be bad for you and me. Do you hear what I'm saying?" John said in a serious tone.

Paul was taken back by John's authoritative stance on what happened. He felt like he was just taken to the woodshed by one of his old football coaches. "I screwed up John. I'm sorry. It won't happen again, I promise," Paul said sheepishly as they walked outside to get into a cab.

The rest of the trip was uneventful. Paul was on time each morning and during the sales calls he displayed the qualities with clients that had MediTech so high on his potential. It seemed as if Paul heard John and took his words to heart.

A Night on the Town

The old saying, "What happens in Vegas stays in Vegas," didn't apply to John when it came to his relationship with Abigail. When he returned home he shared what happened with Paul. He knew everyone wouldn't approach their career the way he did but he also knew MediTech had high standards when it came to their employees. He wondered if Paul would live up to those standards. He thought about Duane and so many others he'd met at the company who he looked up to. He wanted to help develop Paul into an employee who would carry on that tradition. He also didn't want to disappoint Cathy or Bob with the rollout in the new states. John realized it was only one incident and that Paul was young but something about Paul gave him doubts. He couldn't put his finger on it so he decided to pay closer attention.

A few months later John and Abigail were on a date while Baily was at a sleepover with Abigail's parents. It had been a while since they'd gone out so they met up with a group of friends at a local pub.

Around 10:30 p.m. they were getting ready to leave when John saw Paul stumble in with a few friends. Stumble was an accurate word because it was apparent Paul was drunk. Abigail asked if John was going to say hello. He told her no but said he wanted to stay a little longer to observe Paul's behavior. He didn't like what he saw when it came to how Paul treated the people around him. He was loud and arrogant, especially towards the wait staff and bartenders. It was a terrible reflection on Paul as a person and John hoped nobody knew Paul worked for MediTech. That was a strange feeling for John to harbor about a coworker considering how proud he was to work there. He viewed his coworkers as more than just associates; they were almost like family.

When Monday rolled around John was at the coffee shop where he and Paul always met before heading out for their sales calls. Paul walked in with his usual confident stride, smiling at everyone as he made his way to the table where John was sipping his coffee. Once Paul settled in John casually asked him about his weekend. Paul told him it was laid back, that he watched some ball games with friends. John inquired a little more, sharing that he and Abigail had gone out to one of their favorite places with some friends. He even mentioned the bar by name, but Paul didn't bite. That made John wonder if Paul even remembered the name of the bar. He didn't expect Paul to say he'd gotten drunk and acted like an idiot but Paul didn't put two and two together to realize John might have seen him.

John decided it would be good to talk with Al and Duane about what he'd observed and how he was feeling about Paul. There was a lot on the line opening Nevada and Utah so it was critical he worked with someone who could be trusted to grow the business. John also knew he was being watched closely with this experiment. Weighing all of that, he knew Al and Duane's perspectives would be invaluable as he wrestled with his next move with Paul.

Later that week he called Al. When Al saw John's name pop up on caller ID he said, "Hey John, this is a pleasant surprise. It's been a while since I've seen you. Are you planning some sales calls in New Mexico?"

John was always delighted to hear Al's upbeat voice. "I wish that were the case Al. I miss our lunches and seeing your friendly staff. Opening Nevada and Utah plus mentoring the new rep has me stretched like Gumby." John knew Al would get the reference to the beloved green toy. He went on, "Actually Al, I'm calling for a little advice. Our first lunch and your personal story had a profound impact on me. Now I'm facing a situation with a coworker who is displaying some disturbing tendencies when it comes to alcohol and I'm not sure how to handle it." John went on to share what he was observing with Paul. He and Al spoke for nearly an hour and, just as he'd hoped, Al shared lots of wisdom.

He followed up his conversation with Al with a phone call to Duane. His goal between the two conversations was to gain a better understanding of alcoholism and how to coach a problem employee. He felt like he got great insights and thought deeply over the weekend about how to approach such a sensitive topic with Paul.

The Crucial Conversation

Monday rolled around and John had plans to meet Paul at the coffee shop to review the upcoming week and discuss the prior month's sales reports. He knew the longer he waited to talk with Paul about his observations the harder it would be to broach the subject so he decided to address the elephant in the room right away. He'd never dealt with a situation like this so he was a little unsure of himself. That stemmed from not knowing exactly what to say or how Paul would respond. Would Paul accept what he had to say? Would he get angry or defensive? John had no idea. Duane reminded John his feelings were normal, but courage was doing the right thing no matter how he felt.

The truth was, John liked Paul. Apart from the observations about his drinking he saw tremendous potential in Paul because of his drive, smarts, and personal charm. Although he was initially intimidated by him, he really wanted Paul to succeed.

John arrived earlier than normal so he could relax and think. When Paul strolled in, John got up to greet him and they got in line to place their orders. After getting their drinks they made their way to the small table in the corner where John had been sitting. John took a deep breath as he readied himself to step into the unknown. He was glad there weren't many people around. Paul was astute enough to know something was different with John so he asked, "Is something on your mind John? You don't look like your normal self."

John started, "Paul, I have something I need to discuss with you and it's sensitive. Before I start, I want you to know I've given this a lot of thought and discussed it in confidence with a couple of trusted mentors."

Now Paul was the one who looked uneasy. He asked, "Have I done something wrong? If I have, believe me, I'm unaware."

John had both hands on his coffee cup. The warmth of the ceramic mug made him feel a little more relaxed so he decided to dive into the deep end. "Paul, I'm concerned for you because I think you might have a drinking problem."

Surprised, Paul exclaimed, "What? Are you kidding me? Why would you think that?"

This wasn't the response John hoped for, but Al had prepared him well during their call. Al told him most people who have a problem, be it drugs, alcohol, or anything else, will be defensive at first when confronted. John went on, "Paul, I like you and I think the sky's the limit for whatever you do in life. You're smart, charming and have the discipline of an athlete to apply yourself. I realize you're only a few years out of college and still like to have fun but something inside me thinks it's more than just having fun."

Paul shot back, "Are you talking about when I stayed out too long in Vegas? I apologized and it's not happened since."

John shared, "Just over a week ago, when I mentioned Abigail and I went out with some friends, we saw you come into the bar just before we left. You literally stumbled in. It was obvious you were drunk."

"I was out with some buddies and yes, we had a lot to drink but we were smart about it and took a taxi everywhere we went," Paul asserted.

"I'm glad to hear that because no one looked like they should be driving. My concern wasn't just your drinking. You treated everyone around you disrespectfully. There's no way you would want someone to treat your parents, siblings, or friends that way. I don't think you would treat anyone that way if you were sober," John told him.

Paul honestly didn't remember much about that night so he had no comeback. Instead, he tried to shift the conversation. He leaned back in his chair, trying to appear relaxed and confident, then said, "John, I appreciate your concern but I'll be fine. And, what I do on my own time is my business."

With a sudden surge of confidence John shot back, "You're right Paul, what you do is your business but it's just as true that on the clock or not, you are a reflection of MediTech. I would have been embarrassed to introduce you as a coworker. I've never felt that way about anyone at the company. To the contrary, I've always been proud to introduce my coworkers to anyone."

He paused to gather himself then went on, "Look Paul, I'm having this conversation because, as I said at the beginning, I like you and see tremendous potential. So many people have helped me along the way and I want to help you. I want to see you succeed but I think your drinking, if not dealt with soon, could derail a great career, at least with MediTech."

Paul could see John wasn't coming from a self-serving place. This wasn't about getting him to perform. He sensed John cared about him as a person and, if he were being truthful, he admired many qualities about John. He knew he was successful, personally and professionally, and Paul desired to be viewed the same way. Finally, he relented a little, "So what do you want to see from me John?"

"Honestly, I don't have any answers because I've not walked the path you may be on. What I think might help is if you spend some time talking with someone who has walked that path. His name is Al Harris. He's a MediTech client in New Mexico and he's a recovering alcoholic, sober more than 30 years. We've become good friends and I leaned on him for advice before having this conversation. Would you be willing to spend an hour or so with him each week for the next month to hear his story and perhaps gain a different perspective about your drinking?"

"I don't suppose that's too big an ask," Paul said with some relief. He was afraid John might give him some ultimatum or threaten to tell someone at corporate. That showed he still had much to learn about John because that wasn't John's style.

Relieved that the conversation was now going well John replied, "That's great Paul. I know you'll enjoy talking with Al and getting to know him. I don't wrestle with drinking, but I learn so much each time we speak because Al's insights about life are profound. I'll get you his contact info and share yours with him so he recognizes your number. Will you give him a call by the end of the week?" *John asked that final question because he knew if Paul said yes, he would be far more likely to make the call versus John telling him he needed to call.* As John expected, Paul agreed. *Giving Paul the contact information for Al would serve as reinforcement for Paul's commitment. This was an application of consistency and John wanted to make sure he influenced Paul into taking the necessary steps.*

John was glad he confronted the situation and the rest of the day felt uneventful by comparison. He hoped Al would be able to connect with Paul at a deep level so Paul would give serious thought to his drinking, career, and life.

Things Were Looking Up Until...

True to his word, Paul followed up with Al and quickly realized John was right. Al was a great guy and Paul looked forward to their conversations. In fact, he didn't just have four calls as promised, he made eight calls over several months. Paul wasn't convinced he was an alcoholic but over those months John sensed a change in Paul. He didn't know what Paul did on weekends other than their Monday morning banter but he clearly saw Paul was taking his role at Medi-Tech more seriously. And, it didn't escape John's notice that Paul no longer tried to talk him into going out when they were on the road for business.

Eventually the mentoring period came to an end and John relinquished Utah and Nevada to Paul. As Duane had done for John, he promised to be a resource for Paul whenever he needed him. John was proud and had reason to feel that way considering all that had transpired. Cathy Metcalf and Bob McMillen were thrilled that their expansion plan was working. Everything was looking up until John got a call about six months later.

It was a Thursday night when John's phone started buzzing at 11:37 p.m. and woke him up. Groggy, he grabbed his phone and saw Paul's name on the caller ID. Half awake he said, "Paul, why are you calling me so late?"

"John, I messed up. I'm in jail and didn't know who else to call," Paul said, trying to hold back tears. Suddenly, as if a jolt of caffeine hit his bloodstream, John was wide awake. Paul told John he'd been out with a client and his son. The dad left and Paul stayed out with the son watching a ballgame at the bar. He didn't think he had so much to drink that he couldn't drive home. Truthfully, he'd made his way home without incident on many occasions after having much more to drink. However, between the drinks and feeling tired he swerved a couple of times as he tried to keep his eyes open and on the road. A cop saw the car swerve and began to follow him, eventually pulling him over. A field sobriety test showed Paul's blood alcohol was nearly twice the legal limit so he was taken to a holding cell at the police station.

John called Cathy first thing the next morning and broke the news. He and Paul knew what the result would be. Cathy was going to have to let Paul go for violating company policy around drinking and driving in a company car. John felt terrible. He felt bad for Paul because he'd grown fond of him, especially after their tough conversation and Paul's apparent change.

He also felt bad for Cathy because he felt like he let her and Medi-Tech down. How could he have missed this so badly? He expressed as much when he talked with Cathy on the phone after she terminated Paul. "Cathy, I'm sorry I let you and the company down," he said.

"Stop!" Cathy said in a stern tone that took John back. "Nobody is responsible for another person's behavior. I'm proud that you confronted Paul early on. That took guts. Setting him up to talk with Al was more than most people would have done. *All you can do is give people opportunities to change but they have to want it.*"

"I understand Cathy, but I keep replaying everything in my head wondering if there was something more I could have said or done," John replied in a tone that revealed his somber mood.

"That's natural John. I've seen it play out in my life." She went on to tell John about her brother who was alcoholic and died in a single car accident while driving drunk. John was floored. He had no idea.

She went on, "Paul told me about your efforts to help him. He said he appreciated your friendship and mentoring. He said even after the calls with Al he didn't feel he had a problem. He chalked up his drinking to being a young guy who still liked to have fun. The fact that it wasn't interfering with the rest of his life gave him a false sense of comfort. As part of his plea deal he's going to an inpatient rehab facility. I told him we would continue his health benefits so the cost of treatment will be covered. You've heard me say on many occasions that MediTech is like a family. Well, family doesn't abandon family."

John reflected on that last statement after they hung up. Cathy's attitude and actions were a big reason John was so proud to work for the company. The company lived up to its values. Other job offers had come along during his time with the company but he felt some things were more important than money.

In his final call to John, just before entering rehab, Paul said he realized it could have been much worse. He could have hurt or killed someone, including himself. He lost a job but knew he had an opportunity to turn his life around. Had he been older and more set in his ways the change would have been much harder. Last, he acknowledged that being single was much better than it would have been if he had the responsibilities that come along with a family. It wasn't a good situation, but he was trying to look on the bright side. He told John he learned that from him – *to approach everything with a positive attitude and learn from every situation* – during their time together. That brought a smile to John's face and made him think maybe he'd made a difference after all.

As John reflected on everything, he realized no matter how skilled he might be at influencing other people's behavior, *lasting behavioral change must come from within. When someone is touched at their core, that's when lasting change happens. That comes about when influencing someone changes how they view themself and they begin to act in a manner that's consistent with their new self-identity. The other opportunity happens when whatever is being asked already aligns with a pre-existing self-identity.*

There Are No Coincidences

John was unsuccessful in his attempts to contact Paul after Paul got out of rehab. He tried a few times then let it go because he knew Paul could reach out to him if he wanted to. He thought of Paul occasionally and hoped he was able to turn his life around.

Time flew by. Abigail and John had another child, a boy they named Todd, after John's father. Abigail was working part time so she could spend more time with the kids. The plan was to have one more child then she'd stay home, just as John's mother did when John was born.

John trained another sales rep who eventually took over Nevada and Utah. New Mexico, Texas, and Arizona continued their stellar growth, primarily due to John's strong relationships with clients. Because of the success of all five states John was asked to put together another plan to open new states. This time MediTech was looking at Oregon and Washington. The company wanted a firm foothold in those states before tackling California. Before accepting this challenge John consulted Abigail. It seemed as if he'd learned a lesson from his mistake many years before.

During a visit to a prospective hospital in Seattle, John was walking down a hallway, not sure where the information desk was, when he approached a man from behind. The man was wearing a white lab coat so John assumed it was a doctor who would be able to give him directions.

"Excuse me. This is my first time…" as he spoke, the individual turned around and it was Paul! "Paul?" John said with a look and tone that conveyed shock. He'd not heard from Paul in just over four years and had no idea where he was or what he was up to.

"John!" Paul said, throwing his arms around John giving him a bear hug. "Oh my God, it's so good to see you. I'm so sorry for not returning your calls. I had so much on my mind after I got out of rehab. I thought about you often and felt the urge to call you recently. I don't believe in coincidence so it must be fate that you bumped into me, of all people, in this huge hospital."

John thought about meeting Abigail on the treadmills and how she said she didn't believe in coincidence. By this time in his life John didn't either. He said, "You look fantastic Paul. You seem so happy."

"I'm doing great and I'm very happy," Paul replied. "You might recall, I thought about med school in college. I wanted to get into medicine to help people but I didn't have the patience for the extra schooling it required. However, after I got out of rehab and started going to AA, I was able to slow down, deal with some issues, and focus on what I really wanted in life. I came to understand that drinking was my way of coping with the disappointment of my injury. It would have been a long shot but secretly I'd hoped I might have a chance to play in the NFL. Once I started to deal with the disappointment I found the motivation to give med school a shot. I'm in my third year of school now and work part time here at the hospital."

"I'm so happy for you Paul!" John exclaimed.

"John, again, I'm so sorry I never called you back. I want you to know you were a big part of my recovery. It took courage to hold me accountable in Vegas and then to confront me about my drinking that day at the coffee shop. I sensed it then but came to realize more fully later that you really cared about me as a person. I'd not had that feeling from many people prior to you. How you treated me remains a model for me when I deal with people; compassion and honesty."

John was blown away and didn't know what to say other than, "Thank you Paul. Your words mean more to me than you could ever imagine." That made Paul's smile grow wider.

Paul offered to walk John to the information desk. As they made their way through the maze of corridors he asked how long John was in town. Before they parted they arranged to meet for dinner that evening so they could continue to catch up.

They met at a small Mexican restaurant not too far from the hospital. In the past Paul would have wanted to go somewhere trendy but this place was small, secluded, and quiet, perfect for conversation. They spent four hours together. John caught Paul up on Abigail and the kids, MediTech, and the state expansion. Paul told John about med school, AA, and the girl he was dating. Paul also told him he'd renewed his conversations with Al recently. Al was never one to break trust, so it didn't surprise John that Al had not mentioned Paul. The time with Al years earlier had a profound impact on Paul, just as it had for John.

When speaking about Al, Paul said, *"John, I remember you talking about influence and specifically the principle you referred to as unity. I get it now. I've not known Al for a long time but I feel this deep sense of connection with him. It's similar to some of the guys I played ball with. Just one look or comment and we know what each other is thinking and feeling. It's a deep kinship, more than friends, and we would do anything for one another. I feel that way about you too. Thank you for introducing me to Al."*

As the night ended and they got ready to part ways Paul put out his hand to shake John's. Uncharacteristically, John grabbed Paul's hand, pulled him in for a hug and said, "I love you like a brother." They each had tears of joy in their eyes as they embraced.

John left with a renewed sense of energy. More than ever, he saw his opportunity to impact people on a professional and personal level. *That became his new driving force – professional success and personal happiness for everyone he came in contact with* – and he had Paul to thank for clarifying it.

The Student Becomes the Teacher

The HQ Offer

It had been quite a few years since Cathy Metcalf asked John to come to the home office to meet with CEO Bob McMillen to formulate plans to introduce MediTech into new states out West. She was so impressed with John's preparation and how he dealt with Bob that she planted the seed about having John train others someday. With John's help Oregon and Washington were up and running and a newly trained sales rep was in place. It was mid-December, work was slowing down with the year coming to a close so Cathy felt now was the right time to follow up with John about coming to North Carolina.

She dialed him up, and as was her custom she started out by asking, "John, got a minute?"

John replied in his usual fashion, "Cathy, for you I have two minutes!"

She laughed and replied, "Sold...again!"

"John, do you remember our conversation many years ago after you and I met with Bob about the idea of state expansion in the West?" she asked.

"I do remember meeting in your office afterwards but not all the details," he confessed.

Cathy went on, "I remember it well because I was amazed at how prepared and poised you were for your first meeting with Bob. Do you recall me saying once we got Utah and Nevada up and running I'd like you to come back East to do some training?"

John said, "Honestly, I'd forgotten all about that between the expansion into Nevada and Utah, the drama with Paul, then leaping into Washington and Oregon."

"Associates at every level, in every position, could benefit from your approach to people. I discussed this with Bob and we both think it would be a great career move for you to come to North Carolina and work in the home office. In fact, Bob is sitting here with me right now."

Bob chimed in with his deep, authoritative voice, "Hello John. We're excited to have you join us in the headquarters." His statement was an assumptive close, as if John had already agreed to the opportunity.

Taken back, and suddenly a little unsure of himself, John replied, "Bob and Cathy, I'm flattered but honestly, I've never been in a teaching position before. I wouldn't know where to start." He was looking for a little wiggle room.

Cathy, knowing John well and sensing a difference in his tone, tried to reassure him, "Don't worry John, you won't be alone. We have a small team of learning professionals you'll be working with. Managing people and the exposure to the executive team would be great for your career." She paused, then went on, "And here's why we think this is so important...I plan to retire in a couple of years. Bob and I think you would be the perfect person to take over when I step down."

Again, Bob chimed in, "Yes John, based on what I've seen and with Cathy's mentoring I know you'll have what it takes to lead MediTech sales and marketing when she steps away. So, what do you say?"

John was stunned at Cathy's news. He'd been with the company for a dozen years and she'd been his only boss. He couldn't imagine MediTech without her and had a hard time seeing himself filling her shoes. When he jokingly said that, trying to diffuse the situation, she quickly replied, "Pumps aren't your style, and your feet are way too big."

Still feeling a little hemmed in, but not wanting to seem indecisive in front of two people who saw him as senior leadership potential, he blurted out, "I'd be honored." At that moment he felt something in the pit of his stomach. He'd made another decision without consulting Abigail and this one had huge implications for the family because it would entail moving to Charlotte.

He called Cathy later that afternoon. "Cathy, I want to talk about our conversation earlier today. I think I got ahead of myself by saying yes to your offer. I was caught off guard with Bob on the call. He seemed to assume I'd already said yes so I felt like I couldn't tell him I needed to talk it over with Abigail before making a decision. This is a lot to absorb and will entail uprooting our family. I need some time to process this and discuss it with Abigail. Can I get back to you in a couple of days with a firm decision?"

"John, it wasn't my intention to put you on the spot like that. I thought having Bob on the call would show you how much we think of you. I'm sorry it came off the way it did and that Bob put you on the spot. He has a habit of doing that, looking for quick decisions. Discuss it with Abigail and I'll hold Bob at bay," she said.

John was relieved as they hung up, but he wasn't looking forward to the conversation with Abigail.

Another Difficult Conversation

John decided it was best to talk with Abigail right away. It was late afternoon, about an hour after he'd hung up from the second call with Cathy, when he asked Abigail to join him in the family room. The Christmas tree and all the holiday decorations were up so the room had a warm, cozy feel.

Abigail was in good spirits because she loved the holiday season. She innocently asked, "It sounded like you were talking to Cathy when I walked by your office earlier. What's up?"

John immediately told her about the offer, but not his response to Bob. He wanted to see Abigail's reaction to the promotion and more importantly, the move. They began their conversation about the opportunity presented to John. They realized it was recognition of his success and a chance to move up with an organization he loved being part of. Becoming a senior level executive at an organization like MediTech was something John had aspired to since college. Then, before going any further John said, "Abigail, there's something I have to tell you." He went on to detail the conversation with Cathy and how Bob's surprise presence on the call impacted him. Then he got to the heart of the matter, "Because of the pressure, before I realized it, in response to the offer I told Bob and Cathy I'd be honored."

Abigail's face fell at that statement and John's heart sank. She told him she would have supported whatever he felt was best for his career and the family, but she wanted to be part of the decision. The conversation reminded them of the talk they had years before when John agreed to open new states and train a sales rep without consulting her first.

Hearing the disappointment in her voice John said, "I understand how you feel. I know you would have gone along with whatever I thought best for all of us. I didn't want to simply tell you about the offer and get your okay without telling you that I'd already accepted the job. That would have been intentionally deceitful. I hope you can understand why I made the mistake I did."

She wasn't about to tell him no at that point just because she was hurt. She knew she would have been happy for him and supported the decision. All she wanted from John was the assurance from that point forward that any big decision, she would be consulted on. He took her hands, looked her in the eyes and told her, "I love you more than anything. It hurts me when I know I've hurt or disappointed you. I promise, I will not make any big decisions without consulting you first."

There still was much to discuss about the opportunity. They loved the life they'd built in Dallas. Moving would mean Abigail leaving her parents and her best friend Mandy. That would be hard because she saw all of them frequently. Together John and Abigail would miss having a neighbor like Bud and the parental guidance Duane and Sally offered. Even after the kids came along they still went to their place once a month for dinner so Duane and Sally had become like surrogate grandparents.

Despite what they would leave behind they realized a move like this would be much easier while the kids were young. If everything worked out as they hoped, they would be in North Carolina for a long time which would mean deep roots for their growing family. John's promotion and subsequent raise would allow Abigail to stay home sooner than expected with Baily and Todd.

Accepting the Offer...Again

As promised, the next day John called Cathy and finalized the deal. She appreciated John's honesty with her about how he felt trapped and needed to talk with Abigail. With that resolved, she was ecstatic for him and the company. Together they discussed a timetable for the move which John talked over with Abigail that evening. John would start devoting time each week to his new role and they would move in mid-June. This would allow Baily to finish the school year with her friends and would give John time to talk with his MediTech clients.

John had built the territory into the largest in the country and they felt they couldn't turn it over to a new rep on such short notice. They needed a seasoned sales rep with a proven track record. John suggested to Cathy that they approach Francesca with the opportunity.

Year in and year out Francesca continued to be one of MediTech's top salespeople. On more than one occasion she'd been offered promotion opportunities in the headquarters because of her success. Each time she declined because she loved sales, the freedom that came with the field position, and most of all, she enjoyed working directly with MediTech clients. John remembered she mentioned how lucky he was to have the opportunity to move to Dallas when he finished his training. She said it was a place she hoped to live one day because she had relatives in San Antonio. Knowing this, John felt she might jump at the chance to take over the Southwest Region. On top of that, John told Cathy with her stellar record Francesca could help open California down the road.

John and Cathy decided to have a conversation with Francesca when John was visiting the home office. He was in for a planning meeting in early January, shortly after accepting the offer to head up learning. They met in Cathy's office and she allowed John to take the lead. She marveled at his ability to sell Francesca on the idea. True to form he'd given it a lot of thought and the offer rolled off his tongue as if he were just having a regular conversation over coffee. John always focused on thorough preparation, and it was a big reason he could apply the principles of influence so well. Now Cathy was convinced she'd made the right decision to have John lead the learning department.

Francesca had no deep ties to where she was living and leaped at the chance to move to Texas. She had been mentoring a new sales rep and it was determined that she would be ready to take over Francesca's territory when Francesca made her move that summer.

With everything settled, all that remained was to make the announcement regarding the changes when the sales team was in town for the annual planning meeting. Cathy asked John to keep her retirement plans and the intention to groom him for her position to himself.

Russell, Ben, and Nancy were thrilled for John and Francesca. John had leaned on each over the years so they felt invested in him and his success. In his desire to recognize each for their impact on his career, and in the spirit of reciprocity, he asked if they would be willing to participate in training when their schedules permitted. Each had strengths and talents that could benefit others just as they had helped John grow.

As the plan fell into place and the conversation finished, John turned to Cathy and said with a smile, "I love it when a plan comes together."

Cathy responded saying, "Hannibal Smith!"

With surprise John said, "You watched The A-Team?" They laughed as they reminisced about the hit TV show from the mid 80s.

Learning to Lead Learning

John taking over training for MediTech coincided with a new class of recruits that summer. It brought John back to his time as a trainee. He remembered how he felt moving into his temporary housing and the first day he walked into the building. What was so new and overwhelming then was old hat to him now. He couldn't help but notice how young the new class looked. Only in his mid-30s, he told Abigail later that day, for the first time he felt somewhat old.

Taking over when he did was challenging because he didn't have time to change much in the new trainee curriculum. He was thankful for Katlynn, the department training lead, because she was on top of everything. He'd interacted with her in the past but had little knowledge of what she and the team did to get all the moving parts in place. This class was one small aspect of all the learning they handled.

During his first team meeting John let everyone know in no uncertain terms they were the experts when it came to learning in the organization, and he was not. They welcomed the acknowledgement and appreciated his humility in saying so. Of course, John was savvy enough at this point in his career to realize *truthfully acknowledging his shortcomings was a simple way to start building trust and leverage the principle of authority.* Any resistance they might have to their new boss melted away. John opened them to new ideas as he shared his department goals with the team. *Leaning on something he learned from Clyde, he shared just three overarching goals because...there are always three things.*

1.   Make the training more realistic and effective by weaving into the current curriculum true life field experience;

2. Clear obstacles the team faced so they could do their jobs to the best of their ability; and
3. Help each person achieve their professional and personal goals.

Of course, the third goal excited everyone the most. While they all enjoyed working at MediTech, none of their prior bosses focused on their personal and professional goals. If brave enough, each person had to bring up their own aspirations to enable any discussion. That surprised John because he always had mentors and coaches who invested in him while he was at MediTech. He realized even working for the same company could be a very different experience for each employee depending on their department or supervisor. He saw focusing on their personal goals as his biggest opportunity to make an immediate impact because he knew happy, engaged people would be productive employees.

He decided to carve out 30 minutes a week for each of his five team members to meet with him one-on-one. It was a chance for each person to get to know John and for him to get to know them. Beyond that, they could use their time for coaching, venting, learning, or whatever else they deemed important. *Leveraging reciprocity, John had asked one thing in return for his time: each person was to share, in writing, the Friday before their one-on-one, their top successes from the prior week, the challenges they were currently facing, and their priorities for the upcoming week.* At first they saw the prep work as tedious but once they saw how John consistently used their input to help them, they became more invested and much more detailed in sharing. In fact, most saw their coaching worksheets as brag sheets, an opportunity for the boss to really understand the details of what it took to do their jobs well.

John also started networking within the company by meeting with the various department heads. Once again, *he had three goals; learn about each department, understand their needs to achieve success, and expand his internal network. He called it the learn, understand, and expand approach.* He challenged his team to network also. The five people in the training department could make a bigger impact than John alone. And John's staff got another career benefit: just as important, each person was becoming known across the organization and gaining exposure to potential career opportunities.

It wasn't one endless success after another. Just as he'd done in his personal life, John made mistakes and the team let him know whenever he did. He appreciated that they felt they could approach him with anything and he did what he could to make things right. As a result, even negatives eventually turned into positives because they added to the foundation of trust he was trying to build.

One clear example of a negative turning positive was John's oversight when he failed to recognize Becky, the department admin, during a big meeting. He'd mentioned everyone else in the department and their learning projects. Because Becky didn't head up any projects, he didn't mention her by name, and she was hurt. She was the glue that held the department together and her currency was public recognition. When the situation was brought to his attention John had a conversation with Becky and apologized. Realizing how important recognition was for her, he had a dozen roses sent to her at the office. He knew they would be a conversation starter because she would prominently display them at her desk. He wrote on the accompanying card, "Tell anyone who asks, your boss makes mistakes but knows how to say he's sorry!" That got a laugh from Becky.

John had an ah-ha moment with this interaction. His working relationship with Becky was stronger because of his mistake and the resolution. *So often people want to minimize or cover up their mistakes which can lead to, "The cover up was worse than the crime." However, admitting a mistake, then sincerely doing what you can to make the situation right can produce better outcomes than if no mistake occurred.*

Cathy wanted to see how John would lead, starting with a small team. From what she observed, and feedback from other channels, she was impressed. Being the good leader she was, she made sure Bob McMillen knew John was performing well.

The Trainee Becomes the Trainer

Beyond leading the department Cathy wanted John to get his hands dirty on the training. This matched John's first goal. She was anxious to see how he would modify the curriculum based on his success in the field. She knew his approach to people was something everyone could benefit from if he could translate it into training. That wasn't always easy because doing and teaching often require different skills. Nowhere was this more apparent than in sports. Great players don't always make great coaches. Whatever your chosen profession, the goal is to understand what makes for success then break it down into teachable, repeatable skills.

Cathy also wanted John to get involved in the course delivery because when he entered senior management, he would have to influence groups, not just individuals. During her career she'd seen people who were very good one-on-one but not as capable in front of an audience. Both individual and group approaches were necessary for leadership success. John understood this too and jumped at every chance to get in front of groups. Each presentation was a learning opportunity. He approached every talk with the mindset of a performer and answered two questions afterwards: *what went well and what could be better next time.* He knew comedians performed at lots of small comedy clubs to test their material before their big HBO specials and he viewed many of his talks the same way.

John also realized how important it was to set up the training using pre-suasion. What he did beforehand to set the stage for a fun learning experience created excitement and a willingness to learn. *Weeks before any training he was going to lead he made sure to connect with people on LinkedIn. He contacted each person personally and shared a video or podcast related to the training to build rapport* just as he'd done when he opened Nevada and Utah. His approach built more excitement than previous training tactics. People experienced increased anticipation for the training. By the time people arrived for a workshop you could feel the energy in the room and everyone in attendance felt connected to John. Those extra steps took time, but he viewed the time spent as an investment that would pay dividends because people would have a better training experience and were more likely to put the learning into practice.

In addition to all of that, *John always made it a point to personally engage the people who traveled to the headquarters.* He understood how lonely it could be on the road and how much it meant to him when he got to spend time with people when he was traveling. To that end, he would make offers to have coffee, lunch, or dinner with out-of-town employees. Abigail helped by her willingness to provide a relaxed home cooked meal. John's *acts of kindness like this meant a lot and word spread quickly throughout the company. It was never his intention to give to get but reciprocity was naturally at play. When John carved out time, each individual benefitting would go out of their way whenever John needed help.* John was reminded of the most famous quote from the motivational speaker and author Zig Ziglar: "*You can have everything you want in life if you will just help enough other people get what they want.*" John translated Zig's quote this way; *the more people you help, the more people will help.* He was building a small army of people who would do anything for him. Many inquired about working for him in the corporate university.

Onward and Upward

A New Mentor

Cathy was over the moon about what she was seeing and hearing about John. MediTech's CEO, Bob McMillen, was equally impressed. About six months after John relocated to North Carolina, Bob offered to start mentoring John. Anyone would eagerly jump at the chance to have monthly one-on-one time with their company CEO and John was no exception.

True to form, after their initial meeting to set expectations, John always came ready with topics he wanted to learn about. John was so full of questions that it was rare when he and Bob made it through John's agenda. That didn't bother John because he was learning so much. For his part, Bob enjoyed John's youthful energy and enthusiasm.

When John started mentoring with Bob nearly a year had passed since moving to Charlotte. That meant there was only one year until Cathy's retirement. Knowing this, John felt like he was drinking through a firehose when it came to understanding the company on a macro level. While he was still growing in his ability to plan, forecast, and strategize, he had a good handle on the people aspect of leadership. He'd read Dale Carnegie's *How to Win Friends and Influence People* and recalled Carnegie writing, "about 15 percent of one's financial success is due to one's technical knowledge and about

85 percent is due to skill in human engineering—to personality and the ability to lead people." John knew Carnegie's quote wasn't based on research but rather it was his observation of successful people during his lifetime. Whatever the exact ratio, he knew *most of the success in sales, leadership, and coaching was having the ability to ethically influence people.* He was starting to formulate a model to address these three competencies and was eager to get Cathy and Bob's input.

He knew teaching a sales, leadership, and coaching model with the principles of persuasion as the foundation would help MediTech employees focus on ways to ethically influence people they dealt with, internally and externally. The common vocabulary and methodical approach would make the skill of influence critical to the success of each individual and the organization.

A Tough Nut

It would be misleading to think that everyone was enamored with John as soon as they met him. Nobody gets what they want all the time, and everyone has challenging people in their lives. John was no exception and ran into a tough nut shortly after coming to the home office.

Braedon Stanton worked in accounting and was familiar with John because of his sales success in the field. Braedon wasn't particularly interested in the sales team, but he did see the revenue numbers every month and their source. John's name was routinely in the top three spots so he was hard to miss. But for Braedon, a numbers guy, he simply attached names and/or offices to various numbers such as revenues and expenses.

Until John relocated to the headquarters he'd only had one conversation with Braedon. Just over a year before John's move to North Carolina, Braedon saw a discrepancy in John's monthly expense report and decided to call John hoping to get a quick answer. It was the end of the quarter and Braedon was working hard to close the books. John recalled the conversation vividly and told Abigail about it as he prepared to meet Braedon.

John said he answered his phone and heard, "Hey John, this is Braedon from accounting. I'm giving you a call because we have a problem with your expense report."

In his usual upbeat tone John replied, "No, we have an opportunity Braedon."

Braedon shot back, "Sure, when you're in sales it's an opportunity but when you're in accounting it's a problem."

John said Braedon's abruptness took him back, so he said, "Sorry Braedon. I wasn't trying to make light of the situation. How can I help you?" He said they spoke briefly and he was able to help Braedon resolve the expense discrepancy right away.

Abigail smiled and laughed quietly because she liked knowing John was challenged every now and then.

Since then, Braedon had become head of MediTech accounting. This coincided with John's plan to meet with all the department heads. He wanted to optimize his scheduled time with Braedon in a few weeks so true to form he did his homework. He spoke to people who knew Braedon to find out what he might learn about him. Beyond determining that Braedon was a logical personality, there wasn't much to go on because Braedon's rough edges and "get to the point" approach left little room for the typical small talk that lets you get to know another person.

When talking with someone who worked in accounting for several years, one bit of information he did learn was that Braedon was really into his daughter. He soon realized Braedon's daughter was the same age as Baily and they were on the same intramural youth basketball team at school. John didn't know that early on because he'd missed the first couple of games due to previously scheduled work dinners. When he realized that he resolved to look over the schedule and block the basketball nights. It was good on two levels. First, it made him aware that work was creeping into something that was more important, his family. Second, the opportunity to get to know Braedon outside of work would be nice.

The next week presented an opportunity. Tuesday night John went to the game with Abigail and sure enough, as they scanned the stands he saw Braedon. He was different than John imagined based on their phone call and what he'd heard around the office. Braedon was affectionate with his daughter Becca and it was clear he knew several parents as he greeted everyone warmly.

John went over and introduced himself, making the connection with MediTech right away. It didn't escape John's notice that Braedon's countenance changed from jovial to serious when he heard that. John was wise enough not to pursue it so he just said, "I wanted to introduce myself since this is the first game I've been able to make." Looking at the girls warming up before the game he commented, "It looks like Baily and Becca have become good friends. Well, enjoy the game."

John sat down and confided in Abigail that he wasn't sure if this short interaction would help or hurt when he met Braedon at the office in a few weeks. He was puzzled by it but since there was nothing he could do he resolved to enjoy the game.

On the drive home John asked how long Baily had known Becca. She said they met the first week of school because they were reading buddies. She said Becca was her best friend. John told her that Becca's daddy worked with him. That made her smile.

John continued to see Braedon at the games and introduced Abigail. They met Braedon's wife Lisa but other than that it was only a smile and a wave occasionally. He couldn't figure out Braedon. Most people would push harder but John decided to take a step back so he could thoughtfully assess everything he was observing.

First Meeting

The day arrived for their first meeting. As was John's custom, he arrived at Braedon's office a few minutes ahead of schedule to allow for some informal time if Braedon happened to be ready early. John always met with people in their offices because that's where they usually feel most comfortable. Although Braedon didn't have anyone in his office he remained fixated on a spreadsheet. He didn't acknowledge John until his meeting reminder went off. John knew that was the case because he had his phone out and saw the same reminder. John tried every approach with Braedon to break the ice and get him to open up a little but to no avail.

The meeting felt more like a formal interview than a conversation. John asked the questions he was asking all managers so he could understand Braedon's department and their learning needs. Braedon's answers were direct and to the point. John was savvy enough to not push it but inside he kept reminding himself this wasn't about Braedon liking him. Rather, *it was about John coming to like and enjoy Braedon.* He and Braedon already had their girls in common and he was sure they shared other interests or passions. He also knew everyone had praiseworthy traits and was determined to find those traits in Braedon that he could genuinely compliment. All of this was more for him than Braedon because John wanted to enjoy the people he worked with.

Something else John reminded himself of was that people who didn't seem to have many friends or get much praise build defense mechanisms to prevent the hurt that comes with not being recognized or accepted. You know you're dealing with someone like that when you hear, "I don't need a pat on the back to know I'm doing a good job" or "I'm not here to make friends. I'm here to do a job." John knew Braedon had said as much on occasion because John had spoken to several employees before that initial meeting as he tried to learn about Braedon.

Because of his time with Al and Paul, John knew everyone has reasons for whatever they do. Sometimes they're not consciously aware of why they act the way they do but there are factors that push or pull all of us. Understanding this, he knew Braedon must have a story.

Time to Travel

About a month after his first meeting with Braedon, John was asked to go to MediTech's largest regional office to conduct some training. It made more sense for him to go there rather than to fly a few dozen people into Charlotte. John arrived at the airport early as usual. Travel had enough stress so arriving early allowed him to relax and do a little work.

After settling in at his departure gate he sipped his coffee and did a little people watching. Much to his surprise he saw Braedon walking toward the gate. He felt not acknowledging Braedon would be more awkward than any conversation they might have so he called Braedon's name and waved. The look on Braedon's face was resignation, almost as if he was thinking, "Great. I can't avoid this even though I want to." He nodded and walked over to where John was sitting.

John asked, "Are you on this flight to go to the regional office?"

Braedon, true to form, simply replied, "Yes."

"It's pretty rare for you to travel. What's the big occasion?" John inquired trying to open the door to a conversation.

Braedon answered John, "I need to audit the books for the last three years. Because I need to speak with a few people, the company thought it best I go in person."

John nodded as if agreeing it was a good decision. It didn't escape his notice that Braedon didn't ask him why he was going but he shared anyway. "I'm going to do some training. You'll appreciate that the company wanted to save money by sending me rather than asking a couple dozen people to come to Charlotte," he said with a smile.

Braedon cracked a faint grin that conveyed a "ha, ha I get your joke" attitude.

At that moment something came over John and he decided to see if he could break through with Braedon. "Braedon, *I'm going to ask you something and if you're not comfortable answering I won't be offended. I'm only asking because I want to know and enjoy the people I work with."* Taking a deep breath, he went on, "I see you with Becca and you look like a great dad. You're at all the games, you're affectionate, patient, and encouraging with her. And you're always warm and friendly with the small group of parents you sit with. But apart from that you are hard to get to know, especially at work. What gives?"

John wasn't prepared for what came next. Braedon said, "John, you seem like a nice man. My aloofness has nothing to do with you or anyone else. What I'm about to tell you has to stay between us. Can I trust you?"

John said, "Absolutely Braedon."

Taking a deep breath and looking up slightly, Braedon began to share. "Becca has leukemia. She's had it for a couple of years. We never know what tomorrow will bring. I work my ass off at the office so I can get as much done as possible then leave on time so I can get home to be with her. There's nothing imminent and she may get better one day but we don't know. I hate that I have to make trips like this one. As for the parents, that small group of people knows everything and has been so supportive. No one at work knows."

John was stunned, not quite sure what to say, so he started off empathetically, "Braedon, I'm so sorry. I don't know what to say and I'm not going to give you some cheap platitude about hanging in there. Is there anything I can do at work to relieve some of the pressure you might be under?"

"Training and accounting are pretty different so I can't think of anything your team can do to help," Braedon said.

John came back with, "Let's make sure we talk more because there might be something we can do to help your people do their jobs better. If so, that might relieve you a little. Is there anything Abigail and I can do to support you?"

"Becca talks about Baily all of the time and has asked about sleepovers. I like seeing her happy so maybe there's something we can do there. We'd love to have Baily over. And, if you're open to having Becca over, Lisa and I could use a date night."

Thinking about his promise to Abigail, John replied, "I always check with Abigail on matters like this first, but I have no doubt she will be 100% on board. I'll let you know as soon as we talk. And please remember this, when you're at work, if you need to talk just let me know. You shouldn't have to keep this bottled up except for basketball nights."

Braedon seemed to let his defense down, smiled and said, "Thank you John. I feel like some pressure has been relieved. It's hard to carry this burden every day."

Before they boarded John said, "Braedon, I have a couple of questions before we get on the plane. First, are you okay with me sharing Becca's condition with Abigail?"

"Thanks for asking. Yes, when I asked you to keep it in confidence I assumed you would tell Abigail, especially since I mentioned the sleepovers. What's your other question?" Braedon asked, showing an attention to detail that John hadn't noticed before but would have expected from an accountant.

Nearing the front of the passenger line John said, "Would you be okay with Abigail and I sitting with you and your friends at the game? They look like nice people and we'd like to meet people outside of MediTech."

Braedon's countenance was much friendlier and he replied, "We would enjoy that. You'll like them. Great parents, great people, great friends." With that they showed their boarding passes to the gate agent then made their way down the walkway to board their flight.

Noticeable Changes

After that trip John saw a noticeable change in Braedon around the office. Braedon was more outgoing with John from the day of their conversation but where John saw the biggest change was in Braedon's demeanor with others around the building. He was becoming more friendly and open. People began to take notice too and there was a buzz about Braedon. John attributed it to Braedon feeling a sense of relief at having opened up.

As Braedon noticed people being more friendly towards him he naturally reciprocated and opened up even more. What came next shocked John. Braedon asked if John would attend a department meeting for the accounting area which John was happy to do. He asked Braedon if he wanted him to talk about something specific from a learning perspective. Braedon declined and said he just wanted John there for support and feedback. John replied in a slightly perplexed tone, "Okay."

The meeting started like any other. John was there a few minutes early, greeting people as they filtered in. People were chatting as they settled in and waited for Braedon. As was his custom, he came in just moments before the meeting was about to begin. However, a couple of things stood out to the dozen or so associates in the room. First, Braedon had not prepared an agenda which was unheard of for him. The other noticeable difference was, rather than focused and straight to the point, Braedon seemed nervous.

Braedon started talking and right away his voice cracked a little which caused concern from everyone. "I owe all of you an apology. I've not been a good boss or coworker. I've certainly not been some-one that I'd want to work with or for. I'm sorry and hopefully you've seen some positive changes lately. I've been carrying a heavy burden. I didn't realize how heavy it was until I let go of some of it several weeks ago. That's because of John Andrews and that's why I invited him to join us today."

John was surprised and his face showed it. He was momentarily embarrassed as all heads turned towards him. It was as if everyone looked at him and thought, "Did you cast a spell on Braedon?" John quickly got a sense of where this was going and said, "Braedon, I'm thankful we met."

Braedon composed himself and went on, "John was being himself, trying to get to know me and I was keeping him at arm's length, much like I've done with all of you. Then he asked a question and gave me the freedom to answer or not. He said he'd seen me with Becca and that I looked like a great dad. That comment almost broke me. Then he said I was always warm and friendly with a small group of parents Lisa and I sat with at basketball games. However, he noted apart from that I was hard to get to know, especially here at work."

Pausing again to gather himself, he continued, "It was then that I opened up, telling him Becca's had leukemia for several years." Everyone's countenance changed in that moment and you could feel shock and, more importantly, the empathy they had for Braedon's situation.

He went on, "Once I shared that I felt free to be the person I used to be. I don't want to just feel free around John and a few others, so I decided to be open with all of you. I work with you every day so you've no doubt wondered about me and my behavior. That will change going forward, I promise. All I ask is that you remember what's going on with me and my family. It's never an excuse for being prickly but your understanding would mean a lot."

As the meeting wrapped up, each person went up to Braedon to thank him for his honesty and to show support. There were hugs and quite a few tears were shed.

John stuck around to tell Braedon how proud he was of him and the courage it took to be so vulnerable. He also said he was honored to have been the catalyst. Braedon thanked him again and gave him a hug.

That night, John shared what happened with Abigail. He was humbled thinking about the impact he'd had on Braedon. It was reminiscent of his time with Paul. He felt an indescribable joy inside and told Abigail, "I really think I understand how Bud feels when he helps people. *The joy that comes from helping is the reward.*"

The New VP

Planning the Transition

John's two years leading learning and acting as Cathy's apprentice flew by. He was so immersed in learning about learning, leading the team, acclimating to the home office, and putting down roots in North Carolina that he was a little taken back when, in early November, Cathy reminded him of what was coming.

It was 7:30 a.m. and they were in the cafe each grabbing a cup of coffee before the start of a meeting filled day. She invited him to sit for a moment which he gladly accepted. Just as Duane had become a close friend, that's how he viewed Cathy after more than a dozen years working together. Once they settled in she asked, "John, do you know what today is?"

"Three weeks till Thanksgiving?" he innocently replied, holding his coffee with both hands to warm himself a little.

Cathy chuckled and said, "Yes, Thanksgiving is three weeks away and my retirement is two months away."

It took John a moment to process that statement. She'd been his only boss since college and it was hard to imagine MediTech without her. "Honestly, I've been so focused on the day-to-day learning operations that I've not thought much about you actually leaving." He went on, "I'm conflicted. I'm excited about the future but I'm sad you won't be here with me."

Sipping her coffee, Cathy shared, "John, I've been at this a long time. I believe what we do here truly helps people. It was easy to pour myself into that mission. But just as important have been the people I've met along the way. Duane was a great example and so are you. You've made my job easy and have been a joy to work with. I used to joke about cloning you. Well, I might have done it if we'd had the technology," she said with a laugh and smile. Looking him in the eye she went on, "I almost feel like a parent except you're not moving out. Instead, I'm moving on. I'm a little nervous for you, just like I was for my kids when they left the nest, but I'm more excited than anything. We've always talked about replicating the best parts of ourselves. I feel I've done that with you and I believe you will take this company to heights I never could have imagined. You're a special person with wonderful gifts."

A bit overwhelmed and starting to get moist eyes John said, "Thank you Cathy. I've not been gifted in any special way. I was blessed to find a great company and took advantage of the opportunities to learn from so many wonderful people. I think that the same opportunities are available for most people if they're open to them. If I can expand that belief to more people in the sales team I have no doubt we will make you proud."

Never one to show much emotion at work, Cathy composed herself, glanced at her watch and said, "Oh my, it's nearly 8:00 a.m. and I have an 8:15 call. Let's get together this afternoon to talk about the transition plan and how we want to announce this."

That afternoon they met in her office and decided it would be best to announce the transition to the sales team at the annual sales kick-off meeting in mid-January. She told John he could tell his team right away because it would impact their planning and roles in the sales meeting. But she stressed, they had to be sworn to secrecy. "John, *asking people to not share anything is never because we're hiding something. You and I know we have a lot to work out between now and the announcement and we don't want people peppering us with questions we're not ready to answer.* Make sense?"

"Absolutely," he said. It was conversations like this that helped him understand the company and "management" when people brought up concerns in the field or around the lunch table. He began to wonder how he might change those perceptions.

In the days and weeks that ensued together they laid out the details of the transition plan, Cathy caught him up on the major initiatives, showed him the sales plans, and shared the budget for the upcoming year.

John looped his team in on what was going to take place. While they were sad at losing their boss they were happy for him. They were also glad to know he would remain in the headquarters because that meant they'd still see him regularly. He tapped Katlynn to take over the department so everyone felt like it would be a seamless transition.

The Announcement

The holidays were always a big deal for John, Abigail, and the kids. This was their second go round in their new home so it felt more comfortable. Both sets of parents joined them at different times over the holidays, overlapping on Christmas Eve and Christmas Day. Before they knew it, New Years was behind them and it was back to normal life. However, for John it wasn't normal because of the upcoming announcement about Cathy's retirement.

The day of the sales conference arrived. There was a buzz in the auditorium with music playing as two dozen sales reps got danishes, coffee and made their way to their seats. This was always one of John's favorite company events of the year. He felt invigorated at the start of the new year and was excited as he anticipated what the future might hold. Before he took over learning he usually earned several sales awards. He was no different than anyone else when it came to public recognition in front of peers. He enjoyed it.

More than winning an award, John enjoyed reconnecting with his friends in the field. He always looked most forward to seeing Ben,

Russell, Nancy, and Francesca. Because of their investment in him at the start of his career he felt a deep connection and sense of gratitude to each of them. It was the principle of unity he'd learned from Al. It didn't surprise him that more than a dozen years had passed since then and each remained with the company despite numerous attempts from corporate headhunters to draw them away.

Bob McMillen kicked off the meeting by reviewing the prior year, talking about new technology on the horizon, and setting the stage for the upcoming year. After a short Q&A session he turned the podium over to Cathy.

Adjusting the mic she began, "Thanks Bob. As you noted, last year was excellent for MediTech in so many ways. I believe the biggest key to our success is all of you in this room. You ethically influence our physician network to realize MediTech products are in the best interests of their patients. That's the reason our sales continue to exceed projections. Thank you! I'm truly grateful for each of you and I've never been more excited about our future. My excitement is not just because of our sales strategy or technology. Lots of companies have good strategies and products. Our special success comes down to our people. Having the right people with the right skills and proper motivation is what it takes. A good leader can help multiply those, but I don't think I'm the right person to continue in that role any longer."

There was a stunned silence at that last statement and you could hear a pin drop. Cathy continued, "As you know, I've been at this for many years. I've been anticipating this next chapter in my life for quite some time. I wasn't ready to make the move until a few years ago when we realized we had someone to prepare for this position. We invited John Andrews to come to the headquarters to lead learning. John got the opportunity to share his soft skills that have made him so effective in the field. However, just because you're good at sales doesn't mean you can lead. We gave John the opportunity to learn leadership, lead his own department, and learn from various leaders in our headquarters. Now the time is right for me to hand the reins to John and begin to enjoy the fruits of a long career. I have no doubt that John will lead you and MediTech to new heights. John, will you come up and say a few words?"

As he approached the podium there was a spontaneous ovation. The applause was in equal measure for Cathy, a leader everyone respected and admired, as well as their friend John who deserved the opportunity presented to him.

John paused to gather himself. As he looked around the room he felt a sense of pride to work with all the people who were looking back at him. He began, "When Cathy approached me with her plan to retire and have me lead sales and marketing I told her I could never fill her shoes. True to form she said my feet were too large for her shoes and pumps weren't my style." That elicited quite a few laughs then he went on, "I don't want to take much time because we have a packed schedule and I plan on meeting with each of you individually over the next few weeks. What I want you to know more than anything is this: it's an honor to have the opportunity in this role to serve all of you. It's my goal to help you enjoy more professional success and personal happiness as we work together. If we can accomplish that together then I've no doubt we will become the industry leader in medical supply sales. Thank you."

Once more there was a spontaneous applause that became a standing ovation for Cathy and John. When they got to their first break of the morning Cathy and John were inundated with well-wishers offering hugs, handshakes, and a few tears. John took Ben, Russell, Nancy, and Francesca aside to thank them for their investment in him. And, just as he'd done when he took over learning, he said he would rely heavily on them and their wisdom as he got his feet planted in his new role. They were so invested in John that the natural response of the group was excitement. Each loved what they did, the customers they supported, and they believed in the company. They felt a sense of pride that someone they'd invested in was going to lead the way for many years to come.

Leading Salespeople

True to his word, John took time to meet individually with each of the dozens of field salespeople he was now leading. Using breakfasts, lunches, and dinners, he was able to connect with quite a few people while they were in for the sales meeting. John knew he could be most effective by meeting in person so that's what he aimed for with as many reps as possible. He started with those who traveled the furthest knowing he could more easily schedule local reps.

There were only a few reps John didn't know well and that was because they were newer to the company. Yet "know well" was a relative term. John had shared at least one meal with each newbie during their trips into company headquarters for training and meetings. In fact, several of the newer folks had been to his home so they felt connected to John on a personal level, especially after meeting Abigail and the kids. John's goal with the dinners was simple: make people feel welcome and get to know them. He had learned the importance of that from Duane on his first trip to Dallas, way back when. However, it didn't escape his notice that reciprocity was at play. He could tell those newer reps felt a sense of obligation towards John due to his gracious giving. *It's appreciated when you take time away from family to have dinner with a coworker but inviting someone into your home is a very personal act of kindness, one that engenders a greater willingness to help when called upon.* This was the case for John and his reps, and it created a win for everyone involved.

While John had ideas on what it took to succeed in the field, he also recognized the value of diversity. He knew it was important to learn from everyone because each person had certain life experiences, skills, and approaches to people that helped them succeed. That was made very clear to him early on during his mentoring time with Nancy, Ben, Russell, and Francesca.

Shortly after his initial conversations he charted everyone, focusing their strengths and opportunities for improvement. Next, he connected each person with two other reps. For example, Pat might be paired up with Stan and Kim. Pat would coach Stan every other week based on her strengths and Stan's needs. On the "off coaching week" Pat would be coached by Kim so she could learn from Kim. In other words, each sales rep was expected to connect with a peer each week for at least 30 minutes to coach or be coached.

John took this approach because he believed peer coaching would allow people to learn from each other and form relationships that would create a greater overall team atmosphere. A side benefit was that those coaching or teaching usually learned as much or more as those they interacted with.

There was some mild resistance at first because most people don't like change. Some saw it as losing time out of their weekly schedules. However, nearly everyone quickly realized it was a good way to use their windshield time. Most enjoyed it so much that conversations naturally went beyond 30 minutes.

The plan was to switch up the groups after six months so each person would be exposed to two new people. Over the course of the year four new relationships would be formed for each salesperson. John noticed a difference in July when people were brought in for a mid-year planning meeting to review progress and receive additional product training. What stood out to John was how most reps were no longer primarily interacting with the same people. Many even sat with people they were connected to through the new coaching approach. That was big because it overcame the natural tendency, just as is the case at church, of people usually choosing to sit in the same seat by the same people all the time.

John was able to persuade Bob McMillen to alter the bonus plan. Because he wanted a stronger team approach he convinced Bob that on top of bonuses for individual performance an additional bonus of up to 15% could be more than justified if certain corporate sales metrics were met. John thought this approach would tap into unity by fostering a more cohesive sales team. Top performers were still incentivized as they had been and now they recognized helping their peers succeed benefited everyone in the end. Bob liked the idea because he didn't want a few superstars carrying the weight of the responsibility for growth any more than a sports team wanted to rely on just a few top performers. The plan was announced in July, which gave everyone six months to hit the stretch goal and activate the additional bonus. This added a sense of urgency to the weekly coaching interactions everyone had going forward. Best of all, *it tapped into the power of unity because one rep helping another was also helping themself.*

Starting to See the Picture

John's decision to meet with all the department heads when he led training benefitted him immensely when he took over sales and marketing. Not only did he understand what each department did, he knew their goals and understood the challenges they faced. This positioned him well to join some projects that crossed departments. He eventually volunteered to lead some of the bigger initiatives.

John imagined everything he was learning was like a puzzle, it was forming a picture. However, because he didn't have a box with a puzzle picture to look at he couldn't tell what the image would ultimately be. He did believe, as Duane had said when John first moved to Dallas, what John was learning about influence would become John's philosophy on professional and personal relationships.

During his days in the field he learned quickly that building strong relationships was the starting point. People might not buy from him just because they liked him, but he knew they would never buy from him if they didn't like him. The keys were 1) coming to like the people he was with and 2) engaging reciprocity with authentic, personalized giving.

The next stage in selling was dealing with objections. He knew objections may be smoke screens, come from a lack of understanding, or might just be a request for more information. John found that invoking authority – his expertise or the expertise of others – was one way to effectively deal with objections. The other avenue was to tap into the power of the crowd using social proof. When people understood lots of other people, or people just like them, were following a course of action, their minds opened up to the same possibility.

John soon realized, even when people liked him and had all their questions answered, most resisted change. Sometimes it was because change required effort and other times it was fear that held people back. *In selling, change starts with closing the sale. Asking the right questions early engages consistency which is a big help since most people want to stay true to their word. Honestly invoking scarcity, what they might lose by not following his prescribed course of action, was also a powerful way to bring about change.*

As he pondered this it occurred to him that the same overarching pattern and principles applied to coaching and leading people. Coaching can be an intimate experience as those being coached – "coachees" – open up to their coaches about personal issues, feelings, and aspirations. That meant *building strong, trusted relationships early on, just like in selling, was critical.*

No matter how much people like their coach, they might still be unsure about next steps. This is where the coach's expertise (authority) and prior success (social proof) are especially helpful to instill confidence.

Finally, even after a coach deals with the coachee's hesitancy, together they need to put new thoughts, beliefs, and behaviors into action. In other words, the coach needs to "close the sale" so to speak. Here consistency and scarcity could be ethically applied to bring about the behavior change that would ultimately benefit the person being coached.

As John matured as a leader and led the sales team it became crystal clear that getting the most out of people meant starting with relationship building. Certainly some people work for bosses they don't like but the motivation to do so is never great. That's because it's seldom the case that the pay is too good to give up and usually there is no lack of opportunities elsewhere for good employees.

People look to leaders for some sense of certainty and that's amplified in times of chaos. John would come to understand this in more depth than he cared to in the near future. Leaders need to define where the organization is, where they want to go, and how they'll get there. Once that's laid out, each person needs to know what's expected of them and how they're doing along the way. Clearly defining each of these helps replace uncertainty with confidence.

Just as buyers fear change and coachees can be slow to adopt new behaviors, leaders need to implement change if the organization is to move forward. The effort required to change, as well as fear of change, holds many people back even when they have good relationships with leaders and know what to do.

The more he thought about these fears in the context of leadership the clearer it became about how John could use the principles of persuasion to build relationships, replace uncertainty with confidence, and to get people to adopt new behaviors. John felt confident using the relationship aspect when leading the sales team, but he knew he could do more in the area of authority. Some of that would come with time and experience, but he planned to refer more often to well-known leaders and experts to give greater confidence to the sales team. He felt sure this would help whenever he presented new ideas or strategies.

He also saw more opportunities to engage the team with questions so consistency could come into play. The more he and the team developed action plans together the more likely they were to own and implement the plans. Finally, he started looking for more ways to conversationally use scarcity to light a fire for action. One way he did this was to stress how he didn't want someone to miss out on a bonus rather than talking about earning the bonus.

All this understanding of people would be invaluable when John's world was rocked two years into his tenure as the Sales & Marketing VP.

How Could This Happen?

Shocking News!

It was a typical late November day. John's second year leading the sales team would wrap up in just over a month and the sales numbers looked to be the best ever based on the first three quarters. Feeling a sense of pride, he was eagerly anticipating the holidays. He planned to take off the last two weeks of the year to spend with family. Over the prior weekend he and Abigail started talking about plans to visit John's parents then head to Dallas to see Abigail's family.

It was just after 4:00 p.m. on the Monday after Thanksgiving when there was a knock at his office door. The door was always open so John looked up and saw Braedon standing in the doorway. Braedon's transformation from several years ago had been remarkable. After Braedon opened up to his team, their offers of help had been immediate and numerous, more than he ever imagined. And most importantly, his daughter Becca had made a full recovery and declared cancer free in July. However, despite those huge positives, Braedon had a worried look on his face and you wouldn't have to be a body language expert to know something was deeply wrong.

Sensing this would be a private conversation John stood up and said, "Braedon, come on in and close the door." Braedon was too fidgety to sit so John, still standing, said, "You look worried. What's up?"

John had never encountered Braedon like this before. With some hesitation in his voice Braedon said, "John, there's something wrong with the books. There's no one I trust more than you and I need to tell someone so I can figure out what to do."

All of John's senses focused as he said, "Braedon, this sounds serious. Why didn't you go straight to Bob," referring to Bob McMillen. Bob was now in his twelfth year as CEO of MediTech.

"John, it involves Bob," Braedon replied, his voice shaking.

John was shocked! He'd worked closely with Bob since he moved to Charlotte. For nearly four years Bob mentored John each month and they'd gone out socially on occasion. He asked Braedon, "What exactly did you discover?"

Braedon went on to discuss some corporate "partners" that turned out to be bogus offshore accounts. Initially everything looked good but after one of the accounting employees suddenly left, Braedon examined some of the transactions the employee made. While the numbers balanced, Braedon sensed something didn't look right. He couldn't put his finger on it at first but the further he dug into it the more he uncovered. The "payments for consulting" were false. As Braedon traced everything, he realized there were never any consulting interactions. There wasn't any evidence that consulting work had been done. Over the last 14 months Bob had siphoned just over a million dollars through a few of the offshore accounts. Fortunately the theft didn't materially impact the bottom line. The company's performance had been so good that they easily paid the bills. However, the real issue was trust. John understood the hit to MediTech's reputation could cost millions more in lost business and that could seriously impact the company for quite some time.

John asked Braedon, "Are you 100% sure about this because if we're wrong it could cost us our jobs?"

Standing a little straighter, Braedon confidently replied, "John, if I'm wrong then I don't deserve to be an accountant because all of my education and experience would be worthless. I know what's going on and I have the evidence to prove it."

John asked if all the accounting records were backed up in multiple places and Braedon assured him they were, just as all company data was. Braedon told John he'd taken the extra steps to detail his findings in a separate file and made sure to include paper copies of all receipts and payments. He traced payments from the offshore companies to a few dummy companies and could tie everything back to Bob.

Together they decided to make an anonymous call to the company's ethics hotline to blow the whistle. They gathered more evidence and prepared remarks they could share with the board of directors right away.

Their next move was to make sure any further payments to these partner companies were stopped. That flushed out Bob. Bob liked to wander the office when he didn't have scheduled meetings so he made it a point to pop his head into Braedon's office one day. After a friendly greeting he told Braedon one of the partner firms called him to say last month's payment was late. When Braedon told him he was having difficulty locating the work orders to match up with the bills Bob got uncharacteristically angry. In a threatening tone Bob said, "Just pay the damned bills! I don't want another phone call about a late payment before year-end. Do you understand?"

Braedon remained calm and said, "I understand your frustration Mr. McMillen but we have procedures in place to protect the company. I'm just following our procedures."

"Either you take care of it or I'll find someone who will," Bob said as he stormed away in frustration.

The Board Takes Action

John and Braedon were glad they'd alerted the ethics hotline because Braedon didn't make the payments as Bob had demanded. When Bob realized that, he told Braedon's boss, Chief Operating Officer Stan Allen, to fire him for insubordination. Fortunately, by that time Braedon and John had filled Stan in about what they'd discovered and told him they'd already alerted the ethics hotline. An emergency meeting of the board was convened in early December. Bob was relieved of his duties as CEO and was informed that an outside legal forensics team had been hired to assess the extent of the potential embezzlement. Of course, Bob protested and threatened his own legal action for defamation but it would prove useless because, when it comes to the accounting numbers, facts are stubborn things.

The company was still in a jam because the year was almost finished and a statement would be expected from the CEO in early January regarding preliminary results. That meant the board had to act fast to communicate what had taken place and name an interim CEO until a permanent candidate was chosen. It was going to be tricky.

Against all odds, the board asked John if he would step in as interim CEO. This wasn't something he could ponder for a week or so given the gravity of the situation. The board's reasons for looking to John were threefold:

1. They admired his courage in how he handled the embezzlement situation once he learned about it.
2. They were impressed with how John led the sales and marketing team and took revenue to unprecedented levels over the last two years.
3. The board realized the number one goal at this point would be regaining trust and instilling confidence in employees and clients. There was no one better suited for this than John.

When Jim Hobart, Chairman of the Board, shared this line of reasoning John was floored, almost as shocked as he was when he learned about Bob's embezzlement. John stood up to address the room and began, "Thank you for the vote of confidence. I hoped one day I might have an opportunity to lead this organization, but I would have preferred it happening under different circumstances. However, we can't control circumstances, only how we choose to respond to them. I love this company because of the people who work here, the clients who use our products, and our mission. We help people and our employees are good people who want to help the clients we serve. I recognize this is a trying time for MediTech and I'll do anything to help a company that's been so good to me and my family."

Remembering his past mistakes and promises to Abigail about including her on major decisions he went on, "Having said all of that, I need to discuss this with my wife because this will have a big impact on our family. Can I get back with you in the morning with an answer?"

Speaking on behalf of the board Jim assured John that was acceptable. Although the mood was somber, everyone came up to John to congratulate him. While it was not a done deal, they acknowledged if he agreed to take on the responsibility it would not be an easy road to travel. To a person they pledged their support.

It was late when he arrived home. Abigail was still up so he shared everything that had taken place and the board's offer. Much like John, she was shocked. She liked Bob and enjoyed his wife Ann. Abigail considered her a friend and they occasionally socialized together, just the two of them. She told John she felt sorry for Ann and their family because their world was about to be shattered when they learned Bob wasn't who they thought he was.

She thanked John for consulting her before making such a monumental decision, especially with the pressure of the situation and the board. Like John, she noted how good the company had been to them and how much it meant to John. She pledged her full support and told John she would take care of everything at home. She encouraged him to not worry about anything and focus on helping MediTech. Despite the opportunity, John and Abigail knew this was no time to celebrate. As he lay his head on the pillow that night he was so thankful that he'd learned his lesson and consulted Abigail because her support made him feel like he could conquer the world.

Addressing the Situation

The next day John called Jim first thing and said he was ready to take on the interim role. Despite trying to keep things on the down low, a buzz about Bob McMillen's noticeable absence started circulating throughout the company. The grapevine is a powerful social network in any organization and MediTech was no different. Christmas was a favorite time of year for Bob and he was always prominent in the office in December. Fortunately the rumor mill wasn't as intense as it might have been thanks to many people taking time off the last few weeks of the year.

John found himself working overtime with the board and the senior leaders. They needed to get their messaging aligned and adjust their plans accordingly for the upcoming year. He was more thankful than ever for Abigail's understanding and support. True to form, he promised he would make it up to her and the kids. While that gesture wasn't necessary, John couldn't help himself because now reciprocity was at work on him. Not only in this situation but always: Abigail had been so encouraging, supportive, and forgiving.

Between the hustle and bustle of the holidays and extra hours at work time seemed to fly by and before everyone knew it, January had arrived. John and the board decided to address the situation on the second day back in the office. They scheduled an employee meeting first thing in the morning. Next, they addressed their clients right after lunch.

Each meeting had in-person attendees but the vast majority participated via videoconferencing. All meetings opened with the chairman of the board addressing what had been uncovered, Bob's immediate departure, and John taking over as interim CEO. Despite the size of the apparent embezzlement, it was stressed that there was no material impact on the company's financials.

After the chairman's remarks John spoke to each group. He had one goal, to instill confidence that MediTech was the company each group believed it to be despite the shocking news. He'd learned long ago that *it's best to admit weakness or wrongdoing in order to gain trust.* Once people know that you're aware you've blown it and are being honest about it, they become more open to whatever you might have to say after that. *This approach leveraged the principle of authority in an authentic way.*

John started, "First, let me say that like all of you, I'm in shock over what's been discovered. I want to extend my deepest appreciation to Braedon Stanton for having the courage to bring this to our attention upon discovering inconsistencies in our billings. New procedures are being worked on so something like this never happens again. Next, I want to thank the board for the vote of confidence they've given me to help right the ship. We can't control circumstances, only how we choose to respond to them. This is the only place I've ever worked. I tell people regularly, I love this company because of the people who work here and the clients we serve. We exist to help people through the medical devices we develop. That's very noble – helping people – and that's not changed. As was already shared, we are not in any financial difficulties because of what's happened. But that's not the important issue. We can make up lost revenue but regaining trust can be challenging. We all thought we knew Bob McMillen and I think it's fair to say we liked him. I had as much interaction with him as anyone over the last several years and didn't see any hint of him being unethical. In fact, he appeared to be the exact opposite, a man of integrity. Knowing that, like so many of you, I feel deceived, terribly let down, and hurt. Some of you might be wondering, 'If we were wrong about Bob, who else might we be wrong about? Can we really trust people?' Those are fair questions. When it comes to trust, here's something I've found to be true over my lifetime – every person you have extended interaction with will let you down at some point. Why is that true? Because no one is perfect and people have bad days. However, Bob's situation wasn't a bad day. It was an intentional breach of trust but not every person who disappoints or hurts you will do so intentionally. When those situations arise we need to address them candidly and respectfully. I also believe we need to extend grace in the same way we'd like people to extend grace to us if we unknowingly disappoint them. I would rather live a life extending trust and occasionally be disappointed than living without trust. I say that because when there's no trust we operate out of fear, the fear that everyone will take advantage of us if they can. How can we accomplish anything living and working that way? For some of you, what I've just shared are simply words and you need more. I get it and that's why I will close with a quote from the famous poet Ralph Waldo Emerson, 'Your actions speak so loudly I cannot hear what you're saying.' We need to earn your trust and I hope our actions speak loudest in the days, weeks, and months to come as we continue to address this, answer your questions, and implement changes for greater accountability across the organization. Thank you."

Disaster Avoided

The response to John's address and subsequent changes were extremely positive. There were a few client defections but those were newer clients who had not yet built any traction with the company. In stark contrast to the defectors, the long-time clients went overboard to show their loyalty to MediTech.

The employees rallied behind John and the company. As John suspected, they enjoyed working at MediTech and believed in the mission. What John didn't expect was the outpouring of affection both clients and employees expressed for him. Almost daily he received calls or emails thanking him for stepping into such a difficult situation. To a person they praised him for his authenticity, transparency, and his love for the company.

Ironically, it wasn't simply a disaster avoided, the rally led to the best first quarter in the history of the company. Not only were sales on a record pace, the profit margin was the highest ever. John knew it was due to the extra time and effort everyone put in to make sure MediTech came through the storm better than ever.

The board of directors had been doing their due diligence conducting their search for a new CEO. Each board member spent more time in the headquarters to show their support. Between their daily observations and the astonishing quarterly results they knew something significant was taking place at MediTech. It was as if the second-string quarterback stepped in for the long-time starter, gained the confidence of the football team, and was leading them to the Super Bowl. The board decided to suspend their search to talk with John about filling the position permanently. They didn't want to mess up something that was working so well.

It was late April, during the quarterly board meeting, that the board approached John with the idea of him taking over permanently. John had finished sharing the quarterly numbers. As anyone who knew John would have expected, he gave all the credit for the record results to the hard work of the MediTech employees and loyalty of their clients.

Chairman Jim Hobart addressed the board and MediTech senior managers who were present. "John, thank you for sharing all the changes taking place. Congratulations on an outstanding quarter. Outstanding isn't a word that does justice to record sales and profit. Given what transpired at the end of last year neither result was expected. Either result would have been a welcome delight but together, well, I think I can speak for every board member when I say, remarkable, absolutely remarkable! As a young man my father told me more than once, 'Dance with the one who brought you and you can't go wrong.'"

Everyone sensed what was about to come next and all eyes turned to John as the chairman continued.

"Like great teams, great organizations need talented people, but the real difference maker in business is usually the leader. That's so because, unlike most sports teams, no individual contributor in a large organization can have the kind of influence on outcomes that a sports superstar can. There are many fine companies in our industry with good people, but they don't stand out in any significant way.

However, the best of the best, without exception, have great leaders. I believe those are people who are willing to take calculated risks as they pursue a vision for a radically better future. In addition, they have the ability to get people to believe in the vision first, then get more out of the team than anyone thought possible."

He paused, looked directly at John and went on, "John, every board member believes you're that kind of leader. No one else could have done what you did over the last four months. You are a remarkable person who's gained the trust and admiration of our employees and clients. We respectfully ask that you give strong consideration to staying on as CEO going forward. We can work out all the details in the near future. Does that sound fair?"

John thanked everyone in the room and assured them he would discuss it with Abigail and get back to them shortly. The cloud of past mistakes had lifted so this was a conversation he looked forward to because he knew what her answer would be.

The Final Chapter

The New CEO Shares His Vision

John was just 39 years old when he was officially introduced as Medi-Tech's new CEO in early May. Employees and clients were ecstatic. Everyone knew the performance in the first quarter was only the tip of the iceberg in terms of what was possible. When John addressed employees and clients for the first time he laid out his vision; "Good, Better, Best!" MediTech was already a very good company, but everyone knew it could be even better. John believed MediTech could be the best in the industry in time.

When he shared his view on progressing from good to better to best he used the example of healthy living. People don't get fit in a day. There are no shortcuts, doing it right takes time. No one meal, no single workout, makes or breaks fitness. It's the accumulation of eating right and exercising regularly that brings about healthy living. A healthy, vibrant company, one where people wanted to work and one where clients wanted to place their business, would come about in much the same way. John stressed the need for small, incremental improvements over time. To that end, he challenged people to be just 1% better today than they were the day before.

Transforming the Culture

As John thought about MediTech's culture, he realized it wasn't defined. Working with the senior leadership team they began to define the MediTech culture, the non-negotiables when hiring and measuring performance. They settled on five cultural pillars. Unlike many mission statements and culture platitudes, what they came up with was memorable and measurable. To work at MediTech you had to have PRIDE:

1. Passion
2. Respect
3. Influence
4. Diversity
5. Education

If anyone on the hiring team believed a candidate didn't possess all five traits they were not hired. It didn't mean a candidate was deficient or bad, but it did mean they were not a fit for MediTech. PRIDE would define the organization and its employees. It would become what they were known for, internally and externally. PRIDE would be the catalyst to get them from Good to Better to Best! Here's how they viewed each pillar.

Passion. John looked at work as an opportunity to give people purpose and grow as individuals. He wanted people committed to MediTech's purpose which meant looking for individuals who felt what they were doing made a difference in the lives of others. Coming to work for MediTech wasn't a job, it needed to be a passion. While not everyone at the company held that view, John and other senior leaders did what they could to instill passion. When it came to new hires, having that passion was non-negotiable.

Respect. Employees were expected to respect every person they interacted with. They were asked to view everyone – vendors, clients, each other – as individuals with lives apart from work. The visual for this was never forget that the person you interact with is someone's mother or father, brother or sister, son or daughter. In the eyes of their loved ones they have infinite worth, and we need to treat them as we'd want someone to treat our mother or father, brother or sister, son or daughter. That momentary reflection could be the positive difference maker in difficult conversations.

Influence. John clearly saw how ethical influence helped him as a sales rep then as a leader. But this skill wasn't limited to just those roles. Every employee had to influence a host of people on a daily basis. According to one piece of research he'd seen, non-salespeople spent an average of 40% of their workday trying to influence, persuade, or convince people to take certain actions. He'd also seen a stat that said the wisest managers spend about 80% of their time influencing their teams and others. He knew from firsthand experience how much he used influence in his personal life. He viewed the skill of ethical influence as critical for professional success and extremely important when it came to personal happiness. Ethical influence would be how MediTech interacted with every stakeholder.

Diversity. John learned as much from Russell as anyone when it came to sales. That relationship opened his eyes to the reality that people from different backgrounds bring different experiences and perspectives to every discussion. Those diverse viewpoints often help a company in ways never imagined before. He realized what got MediTech to this point might not be what propels the company to the next level so they couldn't afford a "That's how we've always done it" mentality, despite their success. People at MediTech had to embrace diversity if they hoped to bring the best products to market in order to help the most people possible.

Education. Employees had to be lifelong learners. If they were passionate about their careers, then growing their skills should be a natural byproduct. This meant training would take a higher priority. More money was put into the training budget because John saw a direct correlation between training and sales growth. Each employee was also encouraged to do some offsite training in order to gain new perspectives. Time away from work to grow was also considered an investment because it would make employees even better at their jobs and pay dividends over the long haul.

To implement PRIDE John encouraged every leader to talk about the pillars, live up to the pillars, and hold their teams accountable to do the same. He told leaders, "As a leader, what you say, what you do, and what you allow will do more to shape our culture than anything else." They were expected to talk about the pillars to support whatever initiatives were undertaken because employees needed to see how the pillars would help make new initiatives a success.

Coaching with PRIDE

PRIDE was the foundation for MediTech coaching. *Coaching at Medi-Tech was viewed as the ongoing process of improving performance and results through timely feedback.*

Something that differentiated MediTech's coaching was that it was not limited to official coaching sessions; although formal sessions happened regularly, most coaching happened in the moment. For example: Coming out of a meeting was a coaching opportunity, a chance to give praise or advice for improvement. And coaching wasn't limited to one's manager. Everyone was expected to give input when they saw an opportunity. On more than one occasion someone down the line offered John coaching feedback. Often it was praise for something he'd said or done but on occasion it was a suggestion on how he might do something differently. Because he practiced what he preached, he welcomed such interactions. People watch leaders and they watched John more closely than all the others, especially how he took critical feedback. They want to know if leaders will walk the walk. When they saw John respond positively to advice on improvement, word quickly spread and it set the tone for other leaders.

John remembered Duane telling him a stagecoach was the fastest way to get from one place to another in the old West before the invention of the automobile. In business a coach was expected to help employees get from where they were to where they needed to be or wanted to be.

"Needed to be" was a direct reflection of what MediTech needed from everyone in order to move the company along the Good, Better, Best vision. "Wanted to be" was tapping into an employee's goals and ambitions. Employees who were growing professionally and personally tended to be happy, productive, and loyal employees.

For each cultural pillar three to five observable behaviors were used as measuring sticks to determine how well each person was doing. Leaders were expected to coach their teams on PRIDE and reference the pillars in their coaching conversations and periodic performance reviews. As John often said, "If there's ongoing feedback then there should be no surprises when it comes to quarterly and annual reviews."

John's approach to coaching the learning professionals and sales team were adopted with slight modifications. Each employee was expected to talk about recent successes, areas of challenge, and upcoming priorities. This was all tied together with personal and professional goals under the PRIDE umbrella.

Time for Change

More than a dozen years had passed since John took over as CEO. He was now in his early 50s and his vision for MediTech had become reality. They had almost tripled in size under his leadership and became a publicly traded company on the New York Stock Exchange. Operating in all 50 states, they were considered the best medical supply company in the country. His vision was fulfilled as they'd gone from Good to Better to Best.

He and Abigail celebrated their 27th anniversary and were blessed that both sets of parents were still alive and able to celebrate with them. Their children had become successful young adults: either off to college or started their own careers.

Despite his success and happiness, it was right around this time that something began to gnaw at John. He sensed it was time for a change. While he could easily stay on with MediTech he knew now was the right time to start planning for a transition. He'd taken the company on a journey and reached the destination. It would take someone new to envision where the company needed to go next.

John decided to turn to an old confidant for advice. Duane was approaching 90 years old but remained active between his volunteer activities, great grandchildren, and an occasional game of golf. Duane always seemed to know the right way to view a situation. He was direct and to the point with John, "If you feel you've accomplished what you set out to do and you're being tugged in a new direction then it's probably time to step away."

John, still unsure about what to do, replied, "I understand that Duane, but I keep thinking I'm too young to retire. What would I do next?"

"Maybe what you'll do next will become clear when you step away and your mind isn't so occupied. I think it's called having faith," Duane said with a smile knowing that's what it would take for John to make his next move.

As John reflected on his conversation with Duane he knew God had never let him down. In fact, it was the exact opposite, he knew he was abundantly blessed. His family, MediTech, Abigail and the kids, all the wonderful friends he'd made along the way, being in the right place at the right time – he knew either God's hand was in all of it, or he was just the luckiest man alive. He chose to believe it was divinely orchestrated.

Jim Hobart was still the Chairman of the Board, and it was late April, shortly after the annual board meeting, when John pulled Jim aside to share his thoughts and feelings. Jim understood John well enough to know there'd be no talking him out of this decision, nor would he want to. Everyone was grateful for John and what he'd done for MediTech so they wanted him to pursue whatever would be best for him and Abigail. Because John was only in his early 50s there was plenty of time for him to start a whole new chapter in life. Together John and Jim decided on a communication plan and would begin searching for someone to replace John.

As another North Carolina summer rolled around, John was feeling a little melancholy at the thought of leaving MediTech in six months. But his spirits picked up when he saw a new class of recruits walk into the home office for their orientation, just as he'd done 30 years before.

As fate would have it, he ran into a young woman who looked lost. He asked if he could help her and could tell she had no idea he was the CEO. He liked that because once people figured that out, they changed, no matter how much he tried to set them at ease. It was similar to people clamming up and putting their best foot forward whenever they realized they were talking to a pastor or counselor.

John asked her what her name was. When she said "Andrea Johnson" it didn't escape John's notice how similar it was to his name, only flipped. That made him like her a bit more immediately. She told John it was her first job out of college. He asked what she studied and she told him neuro-marketing. She said she'd taken an intro to psych class the second semester of her freshman year and found it fascinating. He smiled at that as his mind wandered back to the Psych 101 class that literally changed the course of his life. Then he asked, "First job, first day. Are you nervous?"

Andrea replied with a big grin, "A little, but to be honest, it's more like excitement."

John looked up, smiled, and silently gave thanks because in that moment he knew everything was going to be okay. "Let me show you around. I've been here a little while and can introduce you to some really good people."

Epilogue – The Puzzle is Complete

Early in his career John sensed that everything he was learning was a puzzle. He referred to it that way because each pearl of wisdom he learned was like a piece of the puzzle. He felt if he could solve the puzzle it would form a picture and he knew it would become his philosophy when it came to dealing with people, achieving success, and enjoying happiness.

Sometimes when you're too close to something you can't recognize what's right in front of you, similar to not seeing the forest for the trees. It took a career for John to finally see how all the pieces fit together and the picture that resulted. The picture he saw was a kaleidoscope of PEOPLE. Everything he'd learned was all about people because the people we come in contact with shape us and we shape them. He would not be who he was apart from Cathy, Duane, Nancy, Bud, and so many others. They were also different because of John.

The more he pondered PEOPLE the clearer it became. Then it hit him in a flash – PEOPLE referred to the Powerful Everyday Opportunities to Persuade that are Lasting and Ethical. It was powerful because so much of what he'd learned was rooted in research as opposed to advice and platitudes. It came in handy every day because there wasn't a day that went by where he didn't interact with someone. Once his eyes were open he began to see opportunities that so many others missed. Persuasion, not force or coercion, was the key to winning others over. Done well, it could touch their core, change their self-identity, and lead to lasting change. The umbrella over all of it was ethics. Done right, influence meant caring about people and their well-being. He knew he would not only avoid manipulation, but he would also seek the best for others because that's what you naturally do when you care for someone.

In some ways PEOPLE seemed so simple, something that shouldn't have taken John so long to see. However, as is often the case in life, sometimes we fail to see how powerful simplicity is. Perhaps that's why Einstein encouraged us that, "Everything should be made as simple as possible, but not simpler." For John it simply boiled down to this, influence is all about PEOPLE.

John's Learning Summary

You've read the story about John Andrews, an ordinary person who became an extraordinary influencer. As a result of his journey, not only did he enjoy more professional success and personal happiness, but he also helped many other people do the same.

It's important to note that John wasn't born with any special skills or have opportunities most people don't have. The keys to John's success included his desire to grow professionally and personally, a drive to succeed at whatever he did, a willingness to learn, and the courage to try new approaches. Each of those is a choice you can make.

Below is a summary of all that John learned, the pieces of the puzzle, as he took notes and journaled. It's your reference sheet and John's way of fulfilling his promise to Duane. Sharing all of this with you is his way of paying it forward, helping you like so many others helped him.

The Influence Process

1. Who are you trying to influence?
    a. What are their needs, desires, and goals?
    b. The personalities might dictate the principles you use.

2. What's your goal?
    a. Have a clearly stated goal.
    b. Have fallback options. Shoot for the stars and you might

reach them! If not, you might get the sun or moon if you're ready in the moment to leverage no.

3. Where to start?
    a. Build rapport with liking, unity, and reciprocity.
    b. Overcome objections using social proof and authority.
    c. Close the sale with consistency and scarcity.

4. Create your plan then go for it!

The Principles of Persuasion

1. Liking – We prefer to say yes to those we know and like.
    a. Remember "Friends."
    b. Similarity – We naturally like people we see as similar to ourselves.
        i. Common – When you identify what you have in common with another person, then mention it, they'll see you as someone who is similar.
        ii. Mirroring – The more you adopt the body language of others the more they will feel comfortable with you.
        iii. Matching – The more you match another person's tone of voice, pace, and words, the more at ease they'll be around you.
    c. Compliments – We feel good about people who praise us. There's good in everyone so look for it then mention it.
    d. *The Secret – Focus on liking the people you meet.* When they see that you like and care for them, they will be more open to your suggestions.

2. Unity – We prefer to say yes to those who are of us.
    a. Remember "We is Me."

    b. Unity goes much deeper than liking. It's about shared identity. Think family or tribe.

    c. Helping those we have unity with is like helping ourselves.

    d. *The Secret – Talk about your deep connections or shared identities, early and often.* People will want to help you because it's like helping themselves.

3. Reciprocity – We feel obligated to give back to those who first give to us.

    a. Remember "Gifts."

    b. Give first and make sure your giving is…

        i. Meaningful – The more you can give the better.

        ii. Customized – Tailor giving to the person's likes and interests.

        iii. Unexpected – Giving out of the blue means the most.

    c. Concessions

        i. Leverage the moment of power immediately after hearing no.

        ii. Be ready to concede with fallback positions in the moment and quite often people will concede in return. This is a big part of successful negotiations.

    c. *The Secret – Don't give to get, but if you don't give it's not likely you'll get.* Make sure you give out of generosity and people will be generous with you.

4. Authority – We look to people with superior wisdom or expertise when making decisions.

    a. Remember "Experts."

    b. Build trust by admitting weakness then transition into strengths using "however" or "but."

    c. Make sure people know about your credentials up front.

    d. Borrow expertise by citing sources.

     e. *The Secret – Become a trusted expert.* Lacking either trust or expertise will kill your credibility.

5. Social Proof – We look to others to see how we should behave in certain situations.
   a. Remember "Crowds."
   b. What are others thinking, how are they feeling, or what are they doing?
   c. Talk about what many others are doing.
   d. Even better, share what similar people are doing.
   e. *The Secret – Talk about what similar people are doing.* Not only do we like people who are like us, we're more inclined to follow their lead.

6. Consistency – We feel internal psychological pressure and external social pressure to be consistent in what we say and do.
   a. Remember "Word & Deed."
   b. PAVE the Way to Yes.
      i. Public – We feel more pressure to follow through when we've publicly committed ourselves.
      ii. Active – Taking the first step makes each subsequent step easier.
      iii. Voluntary – No one wants to be forced or coerced so give options to maintain freedom of choice.
      iv. Effort – The more effort we put into something the more committed we become.
   c. *The Secret – Stop Telling, Start Asking.* When you tell someone what to do there's no commitment but when you ask and they say yes, they will work harder to keep their promise.

7. Scarcity – We value things more when we believe they're rare or going away.
   a. Remember "FOMO" (fear of missing out).

    b. Time – If there's a time limit, point it out.

    c. Competition – People want things more when they know others want them too.

    d. Exclusive – When everyone is in "the club" people won't want it as much as being part of something exclusive.

    e. *The Secret – Highlight loss.* We work harder to avoid losing something than we will to gain the same thing.

More Useful Psychology

1. Ethical Influence

    a. Truthful – Tell the truth and don't hide the truth.

    b. Natural – Only use psychology that's naturally available. For example, don't claim false scarcity and don't stretch social proof when they are not present.

    c. Beneficial – Good for you, good for me, then we're good to go, sums up ethical influence.

2. Pre-suasion – Arranging for people to be receptive to a message before it's communicated.

    a. Remember "Setting the Stage."

    b. Attention – Directing attention creates importance because people can only focus on one thing at a time.

    c. Mindset – Where someone is mentally, emotionally, and physically will impact their willingness to say yes.

    d. Triggers – Sights, sounds, scents, and surroundings can make a big difference when it comes to hearing yes.

    e. *The Secret – It's what you do beforehand that matters.* Think about how you can set the stage to make it easier for people to say yes.

3. Contrast – Two things can appear more different depending on how they are presented.

    a. Remember "Compared to what?"

     b. Anchor – Whatever is presented first, everything skews towards that.

     c. *The Secret – There's nothing high or low but comparing makes it so.*

4. Because – People are more likely to do what you want when you give them a reason.

     a. Remember "Because."

     b. *The Secret – When giving a reason, use because...just because.*

How to DEAL with People

1. Driver – Task oriented person who likes to be in control.

     a. Scarcity – More than most people, Drivers hate to lose.

     b. Authority – Share information from respected people and credible sources.

     c. Consistency – When they make a statement, Drivers believe they're right!

2. Expressive – Relationship oriented individual who wants to be in control.

     a. Reciprocity – These folks understand the value of trading favors.

     b. Social proof – Expressives like to know trends.

     c. Liking – They understand the importance of strong relationships to get more accomplished.

3. Amiable – A relationship-oriented person who is more focused on self-control.

     a. Authority – Share information from respected people.

     b. Social proof – Amiables are comfortable following the crowd.

    c. Liking – Because of their relationship orientation, Amiables want to like the people they interact with.

4. Logical – Someone with a task focus and a self-control orientation.
    a. Consistency – When they come to conclusions Logicals believe they're right because they trust their intellect.
    b. Reciprocity – Because Logicals are rule oriented individuals they respond to reciprocity, not out of gratitude but because it's a social rule.
    c. Authority – More than the other personality types, Logicals respond to data and reputable sources.

Listening STARS

- Stop – Multitasking is a myth. Stop everything you're doing so you can give full attention to the person you're communicating with.
- Tone – A person's tone of voice often indicates emotional state so pay close attention.
- Ask – Usually you don't want to interrupt when someone is talking but an exception is to ask clarifying questions.
- Restate – In your own words restate what you believe the person intended to communicate to avoid misunderstanding. If possible, tie emotion to it.
- Scribble – Take notes so you don't miss important points. You can fill in the blanks later.

Additional Resources

Books by Brian Ahearn, CMCT

*Influence PEOPLE: Powerful Everyday Opportunities to Persuade that
 are Lasting and Ethical*
Persuasive Selling for Relationship Driven Insurance Agents

Books by Robert Cialdini, Ph.D.

Influence: The Psychology of Persuasion
Pre-suasion: A Revolutionary Way to Influence and Persuade

LinkedIn Learning Courses by Brian Ahearn, CMCT

Persuasive Selling
Advanced Persuasive Selling: Persuading Different Personality Types
Persuasive Coaching
Building a Coaching Culture through Timely Feedback

Acknowledgements

The Influencer is my first attempt at writing in a story format. Just as John Andrews learned from so many people along the way, so did I. Most characters in the book had a real person behind them, someone I learned from who positively influenced my life. It was an honor to reflect on them and what they taught me as I wrote the story.

Abigail Ahearn – Abigail, John's wife. Abigail is our daughter. She is a gift from God in the truest sense of the word and has brought joy to our lives and many others.

Al Jannett – Al Harris, client. My first conversation with Al took place in the summer of 1990. He'd just gotten out of an alcohol rehab program. We were coworkers but had never met and he was brutally honest with me. He's remained sober and I've learned so much from him.

Becky Puckett – Becky, the learning department admin. Becky worked for me, and I overlooked her once. The roses I gave her made up for my mistake and solidified our working relationship. Becky has since passed away and we miss her.

Ben Blackmon – Ben Blackstone, one of John's mentors. Ben was a long-time coworker who was excellent at building relationships in whatever role he took on.

Brandon Huff – Braedon Stanton, MediTech accountant. Brandon and I had a slow start when we worked together but once the walls came down we became great friends.

Carey Crabbs – John's sister Carey. Carey is my older sister, and she likes bacon, just like John's sister.

Cathy Miley – Cathy Metcalf, MediTech Sales & Marketing VP. Cathy was a sales VP for many years at my former company. She thrived at a time when not many women were ascending to senior leadership roles in corporate America.

Clyde Fitch – Clyde, MediTech senior leader. Clyde was the Chief Sales Officer at State Auto Insurance for nearly a decade. His "Clyde-isms" still resonate with me.

Colleen Beatty – Colleen, airline CSR. Colleen worked with my wife at an insurance agency and is now our agent. Her customer service is unparalleled!

Duane Dabrowski – Duane Edwards, John's sales coach. Duane helped install sales coaching at my former company. He's hands down the best workshop facilitator I've ever had the pleasure to learn from.

Jane Ahearn – Jane, John's mother. My wife Jane has been an awesome wife and mother. I often tell people, if God had let me design my partner I would not have been creative enough to come up with someone as wonderful as Jane.

Jim Hackbarth – Jim Hobart, MediTech Chairman of the Board. Jim was President and CEO of a large, global insurance agency. I've learned a lot from Jim over lunches during our friendship.

Jim Stewart – Joe the realtor. Jim sold us our first home over 30 years ago and we're still living in it. And yes, it was the first house we looked at!

John Petrucci – John Andrews. I worked for John for nearly 20 years. So much of what you read in this book goes back to what I learned from John. He was a great boss and I'm so glad we've remained friends well beyond our working relationship.

Katlynn Henry – Katlynn, the MediTech training lead. Katlynn worked for me when I ran a corporate university. If I could only hire one person, she'd be my hire. She is incredible!

Loring "Pud" Mellein – John's neighbor Larry, also known as "Bud." Pud loves to see his friends happy. Their happiness means more to him than his own and that's a rare quality.

Mandy Radigan – Mandy, Abigail's best friend. Mandy is Abigail's best friend and did live in our neighborhood.

Mike Blue – Dr. Michaels, client. Mike is a long-time friend and ER doctor. He persuaded Jane and me to give in vitro fertilization a try. Without his friendship and advice our daughter Abigail might not be with us.

Nancy Edwards – Nancy Elders, one of John's mentors. Nancy was a coworker for decades. She introduced me to Robert Cialdini's work. She edited my first two books and this one too.

Richard Profusek – Rick the "IT Guru." Rick worked with me and was a huge help as I learned about IT. He took his talents and started Doctor Hospital Data, LLC.

Russell Barrow – Russell Frazier, one of John's mentors. Russell has been my best friend since we were teenagers. He was the best man in our wedding and when we renewed our wedding vows.

Todd Alles – John's high school golf coach. Todd was my high school football coach. He impressed on me that "luck" depended on being prepared for opportunities as they arose.

Lightning Source UK Ltd.
Milton Keynes UK
UKHW011959140122
397148UK00003B/800